BREAKPOINT

PREVIOUS PUBLICATIONS

*Wired for Thought: How the Brain Is Shaping
the Future of the Internet* (2009)

BREAKPOINT

WHY THE WEB WILL IMPLODE,
SEARCH WILL BE OBSOLETE,
AND EVERYTHING ELSE YOU NEED TO
KNOW ABOUT TECHNOLOGY IS IN YOUR BRAIN

JEFF STIBEL

palgrave
macmillan

BREAKPOINT
Copyright © Jeff Stibel, 2013.
All rights reserved.

First published in 2013 by PALGRAVE MACMILLAN® in the United
States—a division of St. Martin's Press LLC, 175 Fifth Avenue, New
York, NY 10010.

Where this book is distributed in the UK, Europe and the rest of the
world, this is by Palgrave Macmillan, a division of Macmillan Publishers
Limited, registered in England, company number 785998, of Houndmills,
Basingstoke, Hampshire RG21 6XS.

Palgrave Macmillan is the global academic imprint of the above companies and has companies and representatives throughout the world.

Palgrave® and Macmillan® are registered trademarks in the United
States, the United Kingdom, Europe and other countries.

Photo compilation on page vii by Mike Samuelsen. Image credits:
©iStockphoto.com/Mikael Rinnan; ©iStockphoto.com/vasabii;
©iStockphoto.com/77studio.

Photo credit for the images on pages 16, 17, 21, 57, 105, 141, and 188:
©iStockphoto.com/petekarici.

ISBN: 978-1-137-27878-4

Library of Congress Cataloging-in-Publication Data
Stibel, Jeff.
  Breakpoint : why the web will implode, search will be obsolete, and
everything else you need to know about technology is in your brain /
Jeff Stibel.
    pages   cm
  ISBN 978-1-137-27878-4 (hardback)
  1. Internet—Social aspects. 2. Online social networks. 3. Brain. I. Title.
HM851.S748   2013
302.23'1—dc23

                                                              2013016797

A catalogue record of the book is available from the British Library.

Design by Letra Libre Inc.

First edition: July 2013

10 9 8 7 6 5 4 3 2 1

Printed in the United States of America.

To Lincoln, Dennett, and Cheryl

CONTENTS

LIST OF IMAGES

ONE

INTRODUCTION | REINDEER | NETWORKS

I n 1944, the United States Coast Guard brought 29 reindeer to St. Matthew Island, located in the Bering Sea just off the coast of Alaska. Reindeer love eating lichen, and the island was covered with it, so the reindeer gorged, grew large, and reproduced exponentially. By 1963, there were over 6,000 reindeer on the island, most of them fatter than those living in natural reindeer habitats.

There were no human inhabitants on St. Matthew Island, but in May 1965 the United States Navy sent an airplane over the island, hoping to photograph the reindeer. There were no reindeer to be found, and the flight crew attributed this to the fact that the pilot didn't want to fly very low because of the mountainous landscape. What they didn't realize was that all of the reindeer, save 42 of them, had died. Instead of lichen, the ground was covered with reindeer skeletons.

The network of St. Matthew Island reindeer had collapsed: the result of a population that grew too large and consumed too much. The reindeer crossed a pivotal point, a breakpoint, when they began consuming more lichen than nature could replenish. Lacking any awareness of what was happening to them, they continued to reproduce and consume. The reindeer destroyed their environment and, with it, their ability to survive. Within a few short years, the remaining 42 reindeer were dead. Their collapse was so extreme that for these reindeer there was no recovery.

I

Reindeer do not typically fare this poorly in the wild. In North America, reindeer are migratory, so when they run out of lichen, they simply move on to new locations. This migration allows the lichen in the area to be replenished before the reindeer return. Of course, on an island, migration is not an option.

Nature rarely allows the environment to be pushed so far that it collapses. Ecosystems generally keep life balanced. Plants create enough oxygen for animals to survive, and the animals, in turn, produce carbon dioxide for the plants. In biological terms, ecosystems create homeostasis. But take something biological outside of its normal environment and chaos can ensue. This is the reason we can't bring fruits and vegetables on airplanes, why pets must be sequestered for months before being brought into a new country, and why reindeer shouldn't be placed on remote islands.

Most animals are genetically programmed to reproduce and to consume whatever food is available. This is the case for humans as well. Back when our ancestors started climbing down from the trees, this was a good thing: food was scarce so if we found some, the right thing to do was gorge. As we ate more, our brains were able to grow, becoming larger than those of any other primates. This was a very good thing. But brains consume disproportionately large amounts of energy and, as a result, can only grow so big relative to body size. After that point, increased calories are actually harmful. This presents a problem for humanity, sitting at the top of the food pyramid. How do we know when to stop eating? The answer, of course, is that we don't. People in developed nations are growing alarmingly obese, morbidly so. Yet we continue to create *better* food sources, *better* ways to consume more calories with less bite.

Mother Nature won't help us because this is not an evolutionary issue: most of the problems that result from eating too much happen after we reproduce, at which point we are no longer evolutionarily important. We are on our own with this problem. But that is where our big brains come in. Unlike reindeer, we have enough brainpower to understand the problem, identify the breakpoint, and prevent a collapse.

II

It is not just the physical stuff of life that has limits. The things we can't see or feel, those things that seem infinite, are indeed bounded. Take knowledge, for example. Our minds can only digest so much. Sure, knowledge is a good thing. But there is a point at which even knowledge is bad. Psychologists call this "information overload," and it has become an increasing problem in the information age. Even the sturdiest shelf crumbles under the weight of too many books.

We have been conditioned to believe that bigger is better and this is true across virtually every domain. When we try to build artificial intelligence, we start by shoveling as much information into a computer as possible. Then we stare dumbfounded when the machine can't figure out how to tie its own shoes. When we don't get the results we want, we just add more data. Who doesn't believe that the smartest person is the one with the biggest memory and the most degrees, that the strongest person has the largest muscles, that the most creative person has the most ideas? Then we hear about the humble German patent clerks, the Einsteins of the world. We call them virtuosos, outliers perhaps, but what they really are is balanced—unique individuals with the *right* amount of physical and mental abilities.

Growth is a core tenet of success. But we often destroy our greatest innovations by the constant pursuit of growth. An idea emerges, takes hold, crosses the chasm, hits a tipping point, and then starts a meteoric rise with seemingly limitless potential. But more often than not, it implodes, destroying itself in the process. Ideas are consumed just like lichen.

Technology may not need food to survive, but it too has limits. Energy is an important consumption limit, and we are seeing the environmental effects of ignoring that. Usefulness is also a key limit: often times, the more something grows beyond a certain point, the more cumbersome it is to use. With networks, such as the internet, Facebook, and Twitter, the users themselves are often the problem. Too many people on one network create congestion not unlike that on a busy highway: eventually the entire network gridlocks. Rather than endless growth, the goal should be to grow as quickly as possible—what technologists call hypergrowth—until the breakpoint is reached. Then stop and reap the benefits of scale alongside stability.

The problems associated with too much growth are as relevant in business and economics as they are in technology and biology. It is often thought that for an economy to be healthy, it must be growing; otherwise it is in recession. Inflationary growth has become a proxy for economic health, but growth and health are not synonymous. In fact, the effects of even a "healthy" amount of inflation can be detrimental in the long run. This is because of the many systems built on top of institutions that are forced to exceed inflation: bonds must grow greater than inflation; stocks must grow beyond the rate of bonds; and companies must grow beyond the rate of their stocks. Few companies are able to maintain the hypergrowth required in this type of economic environment. The effect is an ecosystem out of balance: only 65 of the companies listed on the New York Stock Exchange in 1925 still exist as independent businesses today.

III

This book is not about failure, not even about breakpoints. It is about understanding what happens after a breakpoint. Breakpoints can't and shouldn't be avoided, but they can be identified. It turns out that all successful networks go through a breakpoint, but while some fail, many succeed spectacularly. The brain, for instance, overgrows and then shrinks; in doing so, we gain intelligence. It is because we build up too many neurons and neural connections as children that we become intelligent as adults. Without this process, we could never grow wise. The warning to heed isn't to avoid breakpoints; it is to avoid too much expansion after a breakpoint. Growth is not a bad thing unless it becomes the *only* thing.

Studying biological systems is perhaps the best way to understand the complex networks that humanity has created. This book is not about biology, but it relies on examples from the animal kingdom—deer, ants, bees, even cellular biology. But the main focus is on technology: how to recognize when a network hits a breakpoint, what to do when it does, and how to manage it to success. This book is centered on the internet, the biggest technological revolution of the twentieth century and likely the driving force of innovation for the next hundred years. The internet is approaching a breakpoint, as are many of the technologies and businesses that now rely on it. That is the bad news. The good news is that the breakpoint will bring better things, and we can look to nature as a guide for what those will be.

Nature has a lesson for us if we care to listen: the fittest species are typically the smallest. The tiniest insects often outlive the largest lumbering animals. Ants, bees, and cockroaches all outlived the dinosaurs and will likely outlive our race. Single-cell organisms have been around since the beginning of life and will likely be here until the end. The deadliest creature is the mosquito, not the lion. Bigger is rarely better in the long run.

What is missing—what everyone is missing—is that the unit of measure for progress isn't size, it's time.

TWO

ANTS | ANTERNETS | MANURE

Deborah Gordon digs ants. Once a year she leaves her post at Stanford, says goodbye to her two children, and heads to the Arizona desert with a van full of shovels, pick-axes, and undergraduates. She labels each of the hundreds of ant colonies at her research site, writing the names on nearby rocks. Dr. Gordon and her students also label the ants. They use special Japanese markers to paint a specific color right on their backs. Year after year, for almost three decades now, Deborah Gordon has been going through this routine.

It would be hard to find a child who hasn't spent some time staring at ants, wondering why they always seem so busy, why they march in a straight line, and why they appear out of nowhere as soon as you sit down for a picnic. Deborah Gordon was likely one of those children, but unlike the rest of us, she remained dedicated to answering those questions through adulthood. A few biology degrees later, Dr. Gordon has made some fascinating discoveries.

Ant colonies are interesting for many reasons. Ants have been around for over a hundred million years, and there are about 12,000 different classified species, covering every continent except

Antarctica. They communicate, they defend themselves, they travel incredibly large distances to find food. They are animals of legend—mentioned in the Old Testament, the Koran, Aesop's fables, and Mark Twain's novels. How did such small creatures build such large reputations?

By digging up ants, Dr. Gordon has been able to separate fact from fiction, and it turns out that real life is more intriguing than any fairy tale or Pixar film. It all starts with a single female winged ant who leaves her home to mate with one or more male ants, who immediately die. After mating, she flies out into the wild, finds a suitable piece of real estate, gets rid of her wings, and digs a small nest in the dirt to lay her eggs. She takes great care of her first group of eggs, nursing them to adulthood.

The young adult ants at that point begin to forage for food, dig and maintain the nest, and take care of the young larvae and pupae. The original female ant is now queen of her own colony, where she lives deep inside the nest, her sole responsibility being the laying of eggs. She does this prolifically, and the number of ants grows rapidly within the first five years, all of them sons and daughters of the queen.

Here's where it gets interesting, and Deborah Gordon was the one who figured out exactly what happens. The queen lives—and continues to lay eggs—for 15 to 20 years, but the colony doesn't grow in size past the fifth year. (How does Dr. Gordon know this? She's dug up colonies of a certain age and counted all the ants.) The queen keeps having babies but they either replace older ants (a worker ant only lives for about a year), or they're sent off into the world to mate and start their own colonies. Ant colonies have a breakpoint.

You may think the average ant is somewhat intelligent, as you watch it crawl across your desk with a piece of bread three times its size. Strong yes, but intelligent no. There is no simpler way to describe it than what Dr. Gordon has to say: "Ants aren't smart." Individually, an ant is about as dumb as you can get. Their brains have something on the order of 250,000 cells (compared to the 16 million brain cells of the average frog).

Despite not being smart, ants do some pretty sophisticated things. As a colony matures beyond its breakpoint, the ants show increasing signs of collective intelligence. They communicate through chemical pheromones that pass information from ant to ant. They decide which tasks to undertake at any given moment based on information they receive from other ants. They also somehow seem to share information through time to future ants within the colony; that is, they have some sort of collective memory (biologists aren't sure yet how this works). Groups of ants learn and remember sophisticated routes and can return to them to gather food. They protect their queen and defend their territory from predators and imperialistic ant colonies. They also keep their nests clean and in good repair and nurture the newborn ants who will eventually go out into the world, mate, and create new colonies.

So here we have this tiny biological machine, the ant, that's very primitive in terms of intellectual capacity, but the colony does tremendously sophisticated things. When mature ants act as a group, a single unit, they defy logic. It turns out that the intelligence of ants does not lie with the individual—it lies with the group. "Ants aren't smart," but the colonies are downright brilliant. A mature colony of 10,000 harvester ants has 25 billion neurons, five times the number of a chimpanzee. After the breakpoint, a colony's intelligence grows to a level that rivals even the most sophisticated brains. Colonies can keep time and do complex navigation (without GPS or even good eyesight). They effectively manage issues of public health, economics, agriculture, even warfare.

In many ways, this colony intelligence poses more questions than it answers. Why do ants grow wiser after the colony stops growing? Why is it better for the ants to create new colonies than just keep growing their own colony? Wouldn't the colony get more and more intelligent if it could grow past its breakpoint? And most importantly, how does intelligence come from a network of ants?

1

Of course, you should already know all about networks because you have a pretty sophisticated one right inside your head. Our brains are perhaps the most complex networks but, like ant colonies, they too have humble parts.

Until recently, the brain was truly a mystery. It is only in the last 50 years—with the emergence of new brain-imaging technology—that we have been able to peer into our minds. Before that point, we considered the brain a peculiarity, something unknowable, beyond science, even mystical. Many people still hold this belief today. It's easy for us to compare the human heart to a pump, the eye to a camera lens, and a bone joint to a hinge. What analogy could there possibly be to the brain—a three-pound sticky lump of wrinkled matter lying silently in the skull?

Ants.

Turns out, the brain is nothing more than an ordinary organ doing extraordinary mechanics. Like a colony of ants, the brain is basically a huge network, albeit composed of neurons instead of ants. There are around a hundred billion neurons in the human brain, each less than a millimeter in size. Individual neurons are pretty dumb—each neuron does only one thing: it turns on and off. Collectively, however, neurons are capable of doing robust calculations, making decisions, communicating, and storing information. Individual neurons communicate through chemicals (like the ants) but also through electrical currents. These tightly packed neurons work together, forming patterns that allow us to think, move, and communicate. "It's like they are sending each other little Twitter messages that have no content; they just use the rate at which they receive them to decide what to do next. It's a system of communication where the interaction itself is the whole message." Dr. Gordon said this of her ants, but it could just as easily have been said of the neurons in her brain.

Like an ant colony, the human brain grows rapidly early on. The growth of our early years helps create network connections. We're talking about one hundred billion neurons connected to each other a hundred trillion times. Those connections are nothing more than a way of passing along little bits of on/off information. This is the language of the mind. Combine enough simple messages and pretty soon they become complex: 300,021 firing neurons (neurons that are turned "on") combined with 22,011 suppressed ("off") neurons in one brain region can yield a pretty sophisticated message—"Don't forget to turn off the stove."

But don't think that neurons are what make us smart any more than an ant makes a colony smart. Both ants and neurons are inept without the networks to which they belong. Left to their own devices, for example, certain ants outside of their colony will move in circles until they die from exhaustion. In humans, most of our neurons are formed by birth, yet we remain feeble infants. The network connections also don't make us smart. We actually lose most of our connections as we grow older. The brain prunes its weakest links regularly and removes faulty neurons in a natural process called "cellular suicide." It replaces sheer quantity with quality, making us smarter without the need for additional volume. When the brain stops growing and reaches a point of equilibrium in terms of quantity, it starts to grow in terms of quality. We gain intelligence and become wise.

That is an important biological point and is worth repeating: as the brain shrinks, it grows wiser. Dr. Gordon's harvester ant colonies do the exact same thing. They hit equilibrium during the fifth year and shed off all but about 10,000 ants. Remember, when the colony stops growing, it begins to reproduce—the fertile females and the male ants get sent off to mate and create new colonies. That prevents the original colony from growing too large. At this point, things change for the colony. Much like the neural network of the human brain, the ant colony grows smaller and paradoxically gets wiser. Their reactions to various incidents become quicker, more precise, and more consistent.

Dr. Gordon knows this because she goes out and harasses the ants—messing up their nests, spreading toothpicks everywhere and the like. She has learned that when she does these experiments with colonies that are five years or older (that is, the ones that have reached equilibrium), they are consistent in their reactions from one time to the next. They're "much more homeostatic. The worse things get, the more I hassle them, the more they act like undisturbed colonies, whereas the young, small colonies are much more variable."

After completing its explosive growth phase, the colony seems to change its focus from quantity to quality. The colony itself becomes an intelligent network, just like the human brain. And when you look to nature more broadly, it quickly becomes clear that this pattern is true across all biological networks.

‖

In the history of technology, we have often looked toward nature as a guide for our newest innovations. We trained our sights on birds to build the first airplane, on the heart to create pumps, on the eye to create a lens. So it should come as no surprise that the greatest technology of our lifetime also has its roots in nature.

The internet was created in the 1960s but didn't gain widespread adoption until the onset of the World Wide Web in 1993. It is hard to believe how young the internet is from an evolutionary point of view. Most people can't imagine living without it: a recent survey found that the average person is more willing to forgo coffee, sleep, TV, even sex, than to give up online access. Tufts University philosopher Dan Dennett likened it to an alien invasion in which we were taken hostage and voluntarily gave up our most primal needs and desires. Some psychologists claim that we created a technology that is now rewiring our brains. Despite its impact on our lives and our businesses (for better or worse), very few people understand what the internet *actually* is or how it is evolving.

The internet is, as the name implies, fundamentally a network. Just replace Deborah Gordon's ants and pheromones with computers and broadband lines. As revolutionary as it is, the irony is that there is nothing terribly sophisticated about the internet. The internet is a combination of two core technologies: the computer and the telephone. Telephones are tools for communication. Computers, for their part, compute and store. Put them together and you have yourself an internet.

Unlike ants, the internet has scaled to epic proportions. There are 2.4 billion people online, surfing over 600 million websites. One site alone, YouTube, did more traffic last year than the entire internet did in 2000. Netflix, our online local video shop, drives even more traffic than YouTube. Facebook now has more users than the entire internet had in 2004. Mobile internet traffic independently grew 70 percent in 2012 and is now twelve times the size of the entire global internet in 2000.

The internet handles this growth with a little-known but fundamentally important technology called Transmission Control Protocol (TCP). TCP is a simple and elegant network technique that allows efficient transmission of information. It works by monitoring the speed of information retrieval and sending additional information only at that same speed. If information flow is fast—because relatively few people are on the internet at that time—information return will be fast; otherwise, TCP will slow down the internet. With this, it creates a state of equilibrium, thereby avoiding a risk that the internet will become congested and stop altogether. TCP is the reason the internet was able to scale from a few computers to the billions that exist today. The alternative to TCP would be constant bottlenecks, like a crowded highway system without stoplight on-ramps.

TCP was invented by a couple of internet pioneers in 1974, but the technology was discovered through evolution millions of years prior. In 2012, none other than Deborah Gordon and one of her colleagues realized that ants use TCP to forage for food. Ants are sent out of the colony in clusters to determine food availability. When food is plentiful, more ants are sent to forage; when food is scarce, TCP restricts the flow of ants. Gordon and her colleague predictably dubbed their findings "the anternet."

But TCP is not uniquely an anternet peculiarity. The brain, too, regulates the flow of information. In fact, the brain has built-in TCP filters that limit the rate of information flow. The brain regulates that information transmission based on neuronal feedback. In other words, each neuron independently regulates the flow of information depending on the capacity of the network and the task at hand.

In effect, the internet is a brain. This analogy works on many levels, certainly with regard to TCP. But you can push further and compare computers on the internet to neurons in the brain. Neurons are connected to each other with axons and dendrites, just as computers have broadband connections. Our memory system, with its distributed links from one memory to another, is similar to websites and their respective links. And the best memories, the most popular and relevant ones, have the most links. The founders of Google used this trick when creating Google's search algorithms: they reasoned that they could look at website links and determine relevance depending on how many links a website had.

The internet is simply a network that enables storage, computing, and communication. If you own a smartphone or a laptop today, you are as much a part of the internet as is the mainframe at MIT. Here's the kicker: that's all the brain is as well. When you break it down to its fundamental building blocks, the brain is just like the internet: a computing, storage, and communication device. And so is an ant colony. The internet is an ant colony is a brain.

III

There is a curve that has followed me throughout my career. It is not a normal distribution curve; in fact, it doesn't look anything like a bell. It is abnormal, yet I saw it regularly in science—first as a doctoral student, then throughout my research, and later beyond my primary field. As I began my business career, it appeared everywhere, but I couldn't make sense of it. It is rarely spoken about in technology circles, yet it is persistent there as well. The curve appears in brains, ants, the internet, and virtually all other networks. It is a curve of success and looks like this:

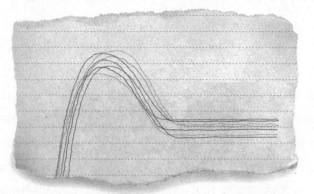

Image 2.1: The Network Curve

Biological networks all follow similar paths and obey simple laws of nature. It should come as no surprise that technology's greatest networks do so as well. What is surprising, however, is how predictable these networks are and how little of that predictability we actually use to advance technology. The biological basis of TCP is millions of years old, and we have understood it in terms of the brain for at least 100 years. Yet when it came time to "invent" TCP for the internet, we did it from scratch, the hard way. We don't need to wonder whether the internet, or any other network, would have developed quicker "had we known" because we do actually know.

And it is not just the internet or even just technology that can benefit from an understanding of how networks function. All businesses, all consumers, all individuals can stay ahead of the turbulence and create an environment of success by understanding what lies ahead. Networks are pretty enigmatic, but they are also predictable.

Network laws are easily understood and have profound implications that enable us to predict where a network is headed. Want to know whether your friends will be on Facebook? How about whether you will be using Google in five years? Is Apple going to remain the golden stock? What's the next big thing? All of these questions have answers, and they come in the form of what happens to biological networks.

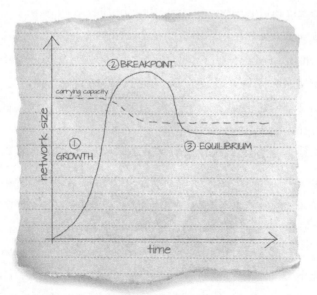

Image 2.2: Three Phases of Networks

There are three phases to any successful network: first, the network grows and grows and grows exponentially; second, the network hits a breakpoint, where it overshoots itself and overgrows to a point where it must decline, either slightly or substantially; finally, the network hits equilibrium and grows only in the cerebral sense, in quality rather than in quantity.

PHASE 1: GROWTH

Internets, ant colonies, and brains all start small, grow steadily, and then explode into hypergrowth. In nature, all species multiply as much as resources allow. This expansion may start linearly, but it quickly becomes exponential. Populations of plants, animals, yeast, and brain cells grow unencumbered until they reach the maximum quantity that the environment can sustain, the *carrying capacity* of an ecosystem.

If you put one bacterium in a Petri dish with some nutrients, the bacteria population will literally double every minute until the dish is completely full and can't grow anymore, which only takes about an hour. In the human brain, we see a rapid expansion of neurons (called neurogenesis) in utero, where our brain size peaks at around 100 billion neurons. A fetus can generate an astronomical 250,000 neurons per minute.

There is a good evolutionary reason for this, and survival often depends on it. The world is a competitive place, and the best way to stomp out potential rivals is to consume all the available resources necessary for survival. Otherwise, the risk is that someone else will come along and use those resources to grow and eventually encroach on the ones you need to survive. The same is true of technology and business: if you don't dominate a market, you will give potential upstarts an opportunity to grow and eventually compete with you. Monopolies prevent competition, which is as good in business as it is in nature—if, that is, you are the monopoly.

Remember the early days of the internet? It started as a network of only a few connected computers, growing slowly in the early days but expanding rapidly thereafter. Around the year 2000, the number of devices connected to the internet exploded, growing to five billion within eight years. There are now more devices connected to the internet than there are people on earth.

It is in this exponential growth phase that most networks die. In biology, species are weeded out here through natural selection. Very few organisms have the fitness to ultimately hit the growth curve that ensures sustainability. In technology, 95 percent of all innovations don't make it through this critical phase. We can look back and clearly see the tremendous growth in the early days of Google, Facebook, Twitter, and Instagram. But for each of these successful companies, there were myriad others that flamed out before getting anywhere close to their carrying capacity (remember Eons.com, eToys, or AltaVista?). When an environment has excess carrying capacity, competitors will inevitably rise up and seize the opportunity to steal it. Just as it does in nature, Darwinian selection somehow selects out unfit technology as well.

PHASE 2: BREAKPOINT

Networks rarely approach their limits in a measured, orderly fashion. There are two reasons for this. First, exponential growth is hard to control, even for Mother Nature. Second, networks often don't know the carrying capacity of their environments until they've exceeded it. This is a characteristic of limits in general: the only way to recognize a limit is to exceed it. It is for this reason that the *breakpoint* of a network—the time at which it exceeds the carrying capacity of its environment—is so critical.

Think about it: the only way to know that you should really only have two drinks at the company holiday party is because last year you had four. The only way for the city to determine an appropriate speed limit is to determine the unsafe speed and then subtract a few miles per hour. How are weight limits determined on elevators? How do we know the maximum oven temperature for a pizza? Because someone has exceeded the limit at least once.

Biological networks almost always exceed their limits by growing too large for the carrying capacity of their environments. In ecology this is called "overshoot," and it's true in technology as well as nature. How do ants know they've reached their maximum suitable colony size? The colony gets a little oversized, which results in too much congestion, noise, and confusion. This is how the ants know it's time to start sending fertile ants out of the colony to reproduce elsewhere.

The brain does a similar culling, by shedding neurons and neural connections. By the time a child is five years old, there are nearly 1,000 trillion neural connections. Through a process of selective pruning, the 1,000 trillion connections shrink to roughly 100 trillion by adulthood.

So in ants and brains, Phase 2 is best described as an "overshoot and pruning" or an "overshoot and collapse." So why is the breakpoint so important? Because once you overshoot the carrying capacity, everything changes. The most important thing is to determine where the breakpoint actually resides and act accordingly. The goal is to identify the breakpoint and reduce the friction that the overshoot causes.

Carrying capacity is elastic: if you overshoot too far beyond the breakpoint, your capacity will drop proportionally in the opposite direction. In those cases, the reduction is truly a catastrophic collapse. But if you identify the breakpoint and limit the growth beyond it, the network will merely shrink back to a respectable level. While exciting to investigate, no one wants to be part of a catastrophic collapse, which often ends up being fatal for both biological and technological networks.

Consider what happened to MySpace. It grew out of control, growing from zero to 100 million accounts in three years. The average user went from a handful of friends to 200 friends, acquaintances, and complete strangers in the same time period. The navigation frames grew from just a few links to 15 in the main bar and 28 more in the services box. MySpace pages became cluttered with automatically playing songs, videos, glitzy wallpaper, and other widgets. Basically, it got congested, noisy, and too confusing to navigate—MySpace grew too far beyond its breakpoint. The

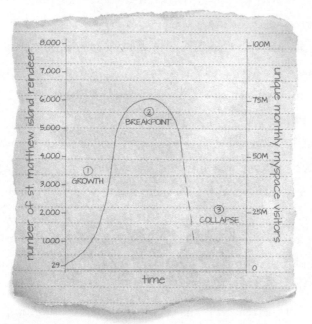

Image 2.3: When Networks Collapse: MySpace and St. Matthew Island Reindeer

graph of MySpace's collapse looks very similar to that of the St. Matthew Island reindeer.

PHASE 3: EQUILIBRIUM

Unless there is a natural disaster, biological networks generally don't fail in such a dramatic fashion. For that, it takes some human interference. Remember, the reindeer were brought to St. Matthew Island by people; Mother Nature never put reindeer there. And MySpace was certainly a human invention.

Ant colonies, various other animal species, brains, and internets are all networks, and as such they follow the same pattern of growth, breakpoint, and equilibrium. They start out small and grow explosively to the point where they overshoot and collapse. A successful network has only a small collapse, out of which a stronger network emerges wherein it reaches equilibrium, oscillating around an ideal size.

At the phase of equilibrium, networks continue to grow, but in terms of *quality* instead of quantity. When the size of a network slows, other things speed up—like communication, intelligence, and consciousness. At this point, the real magic begins.

This last network phase is poorly understood, even by biologists. We are just beginning to learn about equilibriums in biological systems, let alone in technology. When Deborah Gordon first discovered these properties in ant colonies, she learned that the size of a colony remains stable, that it has no central leadership, and that it becomes intelligent at equilibrium. But no one yet knows why or how this happens.

Part of the reason is that people dismiss the notion that intelligence can come from a network. When we talk about ourselves, it is easy to call us intelligent beings. It comes naturally, even if it's anthropocentric. But when we talk about our neurons in our brains, the discussion starts to get a bit dicey. It is hard for us to believe that the human mind could emerge out of something as simple as neuronal firings. For many people, the brain seems beyond a scientific explanation. While some may find it hard to believe, the evidence supporting the science of neurons is now irrefutable.

The science of neurons brings into question the most fundamental beliefs about intelligence. The reality is that if we are willing to accept that neurons are what make us smart, then all entities with sufficient neurons must be capable of intelligence, rationality, and even consciousness. Of course, the term "sufficient" is up for debate, as always. We don't attribute intelligence to a sea slug with its measly 18,000 neurons or to an individual ant at 250,000. But how about a mouse at 75 million or a housecat at 1 trillion?

What about a collective intelligence, one that comes not from a single brain but from a group? If intelligence comes from a network of neurons, it stands to reason that the network doesn't need to be in a single body. It is worth considering whether an ant colony, with its trillions of neurons, is deserving of our consideration. Could it be that the ant itself is a mere part, that the colony *is* the organism? The answer to this question has profound implications for other networks. If we accept that the brain is a smart network even though individual neurons are simpletons, and that the ant colony is intelligent even though an individual ant isn't, we're acknowledging that networks possess intelligence beyond the sum of their parts. And if that is the case, then the internet as a collective unit could also gain intelligence, rationality, and consciousness once it reaches equilibrium.

IV

In 1880, the United States brought together the world's leading experts to determine what New York City would look like in 100 years. At the time, New York was a fast-growing hub of entrepreneurship and innovation. The city had launched the first elevated train, was experimenting with an underground subway, and was on the verge of a major feat, launching the first skyscraper—the Equitable Building. After some deliberation, the team came back with unanimous consensus: New York City would be destroyed within 100 years.

Why?

It turns out that there was a massive population boom in New York City. The network of people had gone from 30,000 in the early 1800s to nearly four million people, doubling in size every ten years. At that rate, the experts concluded, the city would need more than six million horses to transport all of those people by 1980. But New York already had an enormous manure problem. Each one of the city's nearly 200,000 horses was excreting roughly 24 pounds of manure and a quart of urine . . . every single day. With the increased need of horses to keep up with the population, even 20 years of growth would put the city knee-deep in shit.

Predicting the future is hard for a number of reasons. For one thing, most people just assume more, much more, of the same. Long-term predictions are hard, and our brains are not equipped to do them well. We take what is current and project into the future. Or we take what is current and apply some flair (think flying cars). Rarely does one take a novel approach to the future, at least without getting ridiculed.

But there is another approach to looking ahead. Instead of trying to predict the future, we can use hindsight to see if there are any historical or biological parallels. We could have predicted book readers such as the Kindle, for instance, had we looked back in time to the history and convergence of electronics and the printing press. We could have predicted that humankind would one day learn to fly by looking to the birds. Of course, for both flight and e-books, we did so in our own way.

New technologies and companies that leverage the internet are multiplying, and that is driving internet usage to new heights. Most people are surprised to learn that a typical home in North America today generates over 5 percent of what the whole world did during all of 2008 in terms of internet traffic. Think about it: twenty homes today generate the same amount of traffic that the entire internet produced in 2008. The internet is pervasive, and it is growing at an ever faster pace, taking up more energy, more bandwidth, more time. But it will not just yield more manure and urine. Just as New York City avoided its horse breakpoint with the invention of cars and mass transportation, so too will the internet benefit from new innovations, the likes of which we can't yet fathom. Beyond the breakpoint lie new ideas, new technologies, and new opportunities.

THREE

CANNIBALS | BRAINS | INTERNETS

The business of life was booming on Easter Island in the sixteenth century. Long considered the most remote inhabited island on earth, this South Pacific island was blessed with plentiful natural resources and a peaceful, cooperative population. The island's most prominent feature was its beautiful forests, home to a couple dozen species of trees, many growing up to 100 feet tall. With trees come birds, and at least 25 different species of nesting birds were drawn to the island's trees as a safe, comfortable home.

The humans of Easter Island made their homes from forest wood as well. They were excellent woodworkers, adept at building houses as well as large canoes for fishing tuna and porpoises from the surrounding waters. When they cleared a section of forest, they left a few trees for shade and cultivated the remaining land for crops. Thus the Easter Islanders enjoyed a rich diet of fish, vegetables, and all manner of grain. They were stout people, and more than a few could have been described as plump.

Fossil records indicate that the population flourished, growing from a couple hundred in the thirteenth century to around 15,000 people by the year 1600. But at roughly that point, something terrible happened: the network of people on Easter Island collapsed. Within a century, the population shrank to a mere 2,500.

Though there is no written record of the Easter Islanders from this time period, it's amazing what information archaeologists can glean from the artifacts they've dug up. They discovered that most of the trees had been killed, the birds had grown extinct, and the fish had stopped surfacing near Easter Island. By excavating garbage sites, archeologists learned something even more startling: the Islanders started eating *each other*. Where previously there were discarded bones of fish and birds, after the collapse, archaeologists found rat bones and human bones, the latter most often found split open with the bone marrow missing (i.e., eaten).

What happened?

Scientists believe that the human population of Easter Island hit a breakpoint and massively overshot the environment's carrying capacity. While the island's natural resources appeared to be abundant, the ecosystem was in fact more delicate than the inhabitants realized. The large trees were slow-growing varieties—what could be chopped down in minutes took many years to regrow. We don't know if the people didn't understand this or just couldn't regulate consumption, but the result was the same. The people drove all of the island's native trees to extinction and completely wiped out the forests. With the destruction of the forests came the extinction of the nesting birds and the other small animals that once lived there.

Island communities are often able to live off the sea, and Easter Islanders were excellent deep-sea fishermen. But this became impossible without boats, wooden canoes, to be specific, which could not be built or maintained in the absence of large trees. The fossil record bears this out: when the islanders could no longer fish the oceans, they gathered shellfish from the shore. But that food source, too, quickly became overexploited.

The land was overtoiled as well. Agriculture, which had flourished throughout most of the island's history, was ruined owing to soil erosion and nutrient depletion. With no surrounding forest, the few remaining crops were left unprotected from the harsh sun and strong winds. The annual harvest became a fraction of what it once was. Europeans who arrived in 1722 described the few remaining islanders as "emaciated and miserable."

The Easter Islanders weren't simply hungry; they experienced a collapse of their entire civilization that pulled them back into the dark ages, literally. No trees meant no fire, no boats, no walls for their homes, no cremation of their dead. No fish and no harvest meant distrust of their priests, many of whom had previously maintained power by claiming a direct relationship with the gods who provided bountiful harvests. We can all imagine who was eaten first.

The food shortages led to resentment and fighting. The Easter Islanders, prosperous only a few generations before, descended into civil war and cannibalism. Easter Island is a textbook example of human population breakpoint and collapse.

I

Islands are environments with fixed carrying capacities, so studying them gives us the chance to truly understand what happens when a network hits its breakpoint. Of course, the earth itself is the ultimate fixed-carrying-capacity environment. Ecologists rightly warn that our fate will be the same as that of the Easter

Islanders if we don't control the growth of our population and the decimation of our natural resources.

The brain also resides in a fixed-carrying-capacity environment. You can think of the brain as an island, but instead of being surrounded by water, it's bounded by our hard skulls. In other words, the brain is a physical network operating in a constrained environment. And by any measure, the brain is packed in pretty tight. The 100 billion neurons in an adult human brain have the equivalent surface area of roughly four football fields. It's all crammed in and folded upon itself, which is why it looks so wrinkly.

The brain is not limited merely in terms of size. Indulge for a moment in a little thought experiment: What if your skull stayed soft, like that of a baby? Would you end up with a monstrous brain that would make you much smarter than all of your friends? Or would your brain grow only until it hit a breakpoint? Turns out, if it grew any larger you would have the same sad fate as our islanders. This is because of the brain's immense energy needs: the brain consumes nearly 20 percent of all our energy despite being a mere 2 percent of our body mass. If your brain grew larger but your lungs and heart stayed the same size, the brain would overshoot capacity to such an extent that your neurons would start to suffocate and die off from lack of oxygen and nutrients. Nature has perfectly calibrated our brain sizes to the carrying capacity of our bodies—as it has for virtually all other animals—and this is dictated predominantly by our energy consumption.

We could just get bigger bodies, but that didn't work out so well for the dinosaurs. Bigger does not always mean better. Most people think humans have the biggest brains on earth, but we actually only have the biggest brains relative to the size of the rest of our bodies. Elephants, for example, have bigger brains than we do, but by all accounts, they have smaller brainpower. Networks are all about efficiency—not size—because efficiency allows a network to be more robust and powerful within a fixed-carrying-capacity environment. Remember that even humans do not gain real intelligence until after the brain reaches its break-point—smaller adult brains have greater intelligence than the significantly bigger brains of children. It turns out that being stuck on an island is not necessarily a bad thing.

II

The early history of the internet looks a lot like an island. Originally called ARPAnet, it was created in the mid-1960s by the Advanced Research Projects Agency (ARPA), a division of the US Department of Defense. ARPA's mission was to preserve the United States' technological superiority, something the government felt was in jeopardy after the Soviets launched Sputnik in 1957. ARPAnet, for its part, was created to enable communication between ARPA's full-time scientists and scientists from universities and private research institutions.

There was nothing terribly exciting about the early net—a few computers connected to one another by phone lines. Like every innovation before it, the most riveting details remain utterly boring and cryptic to most people: a 1024-bit packet of information was sent in 1968; the first two mainframes were connected in 1969; the first letters, L, then O, crossed the internet soon thereafter; a third letter—G—led to the first internet crash minutes later (so much for logging on). Ethernet was invented in 1973; TCP was adopted in 1983; the first use of the smiley face :-) came in that same year.

Fast forward to 1990 and the US Department of Defense decided to move its classified information to a different network and passed responsibility for ARPAnet to the National Science Foundation (NSF), which merged ARPAnet with its own NSFnet. Most historians agree that the NSF was a good steward of the network of networks. It doubled in size every seven months and grew to 50,000 networks, including 4,000 institutions, at its peak. The internet grew, but it was still ultimately controlled by the US government, and nothing can be more limiting to a network than government control.

The government was under tremendous pressure to allow commercial interests to participate in its network, so the NSF executed plans to relinquish control to private industry starting in 1994. It swiftly funded private contracts for the creation of four Internet Exchange Points (IXPs)—one each in California, New York, Chicago, and Washington, DC. Then, in 1995, the NSFnet was officially decommissioned, and the internet as we know it was born.

No longer an island bounded by government regulations, the internet exploded into its exponential growth phase. It grew from a couple hundred thousand university and government users in early 1995 to over 16 million users across all industries by the end of 1995. That number more than doubled the following year. Within five years, the number was over 300 million. And we broke a billion users a mere ten years later. Today the number is an astronomical 2.4 billion users, or roughly 34 percent of the world's population.

Just look at the sheer physicality of the internet. There are now hundreds of thousands of feet of fiber-optic cable running below our feet and across our oceans. Look at the devices we've connected. A quick view at a desk covered with with laptops, tablets, and smartphones makes it clear that we are not talking about one device per person, as was the case less than a decade ago. In 2012 the number of devices exceeded 9 billion (well over the number of people on earth), and Cisco predicts the number will skyrocket to 50 billion devices by 2020. That number is likely understated by a factor of 4.

These devices include many things you may not have considered before. Some cows, for example, are more connected than most people. A company called Sparked creates chips for cows that, when implanted, transmit over 200 MB of data per year regarding the cow's health and location. Ankle bracelets on female cows can even determine when they're in heat and send an alert to the farmer (or the bulls) that it's time for insemination.

If you have a car built in the last couple of years, chances are there's a portal online where you can log in to view your car's maintenance needs as determined by sensors on various components. Several insurance companies offer a safe driver discount if you allow them to implant a chip in your car that sends the company information about your driving habits.

Similarly, produce farms on the cutting edge have sensors that measure various patches of soil for appropriate moisture and nutrients. Most send that information to the farmer; some send it straight to a fertilizing robot that automatically spreads more water or fertilizer to that portion of soil. CyberRain is an internet sprinkler system for the home that doesn't water your yard if the forecast calls for rain. Some of the newest refrigerators are connected to the internet and can tell you when the milk's gone bad.

Some of us have internet devices within our own bodies. For those with severe gastro-intestinal problems, internet-enabled nano-cameras relay information about potential digestive diseases. A high-risk patient can wear sensors that feed his doctor data on blood pressure and heart rate, effectively providing an early warning system for heart failure. And BrainGate is a microchip that sits in the brain and allows people to interact with the internet using nothing but their thoughts.

All of these devices (and animals) are as much a part of the internet as you and your laptop. With growth in the number of devices comes a corresponding upsurge in internet traffic, which is probably the best way to measure the size of the internet. So how big is it? It's monstrous and growing more so. Remember, twenty homes today produce the same output in a year that the entire world generated in 2008. Every single hour in 2011, we generated enough traffic to fill 7 million DVDs, and by 2015 that number will increase four-fold. So why hasn't the internet hit its breakpoint?

III

Islands give us great insights into networks for obvious reasons: external influence is limited, and the population can't simply pick up and move on to a better place. Remember that the St. Matthew Island reindeer met the same fate as the Easter Islanders. But when not bound by an island, sometimes a network gets the chance to move to a place with a higher carrying capacity. Reindeer and humans can migrate, after all, and the same is true for technologies, although those network migrations happen through innovation.

Like all networks in a growth phase, the internet appears to be boundless. But the internet is a physical network, subject to physical limits. In our world of wireless computers, smartphones, tablets, and cloud storage, it's easy for us to forget this. The internet is bound by the width of cables, the amount of energy available, and the capacity of routers and switches. So it is remarkable that we have gone from two to almost ten billion internet-connected devices in a mere half century and still have not hit a breakpoint.

In 1995, just as the internet was entering hypergrowth, many pundits were convinced it would collapse under the weight of that growth. Bob Metcalfe, inventor of Ethernet and the namesake of the networking law "bigger is better," went so far as to say that it would "soon go spectacularly supernova and in 1996 catastrophically collapse." Metcalfe gave 11 key reasons, including the rate of growth, the amount of spam online, and the limits of available bandwidth. Many people at the time agreed with him but, of course, the internet did not collapse. Yet Metcalfe was largely correct: the internet was growing too fast, well beyond its carrying capacity.

Traffic was simply too heavy. Consider America Online (AOL), the largest internet service provider at the time. In 1994, AOL openly admitted that it could not handle the load or demand of the internet. It started limiting the number of users online during peak times, almost begging customers to switch to competitors. The problems culminated in August 1996 with a huge outage that affected six million AOL users and ultimately forced AOL to refund millions of dollars to angry customers. Clearly, the population of the internet had overshot the carrying capacity of its environment—its bandwidth. Yet rather than imploding, the internet somehow continued to grow, with more people spending more time on the internet and creating even more traffic. The internet continued to accelerate, defying logic.

The internet continues to grow because we keep moving it to new environments with increased carrying capacities. The biological equivalent would be if the reindeer herd, having eaten all the lichen on St. Matthew Island, swam to a nearby island that had more lichen, and then continued to grow their population. It's like a crab finding a larger shell or a brain if it could transcend the skull. In the non-biological world, Ponzi schemes are networked so that each successive scam increases the carrying capacity so as to avoid reaching a breakpoint (though, like any fixed environment, it is only a matter of time before the house of cards comes crashing down and somebody goes to jail). With the internet, we've loaded everything up and moved to a bigger island—and we've done it about a half dozen times.

Most of us still remember dialing up in the 1990s with the accompanying sounds of screeching and static. The early internet relied exclusively on the telephone network, which was built to transmit analog data. Your computer was connected with a phone cable to your modem, which translated digital data to analog data and then sent that analog data into your phone jack. When you "dialed in," your call was answered by your internet service provider, which enabled data switching back and forth through your modem. Modems were slow, excruciatingly so by modern standards. In 1991, modems worked at a speed of 14.4 kilobits per second (kbps). By 1996, the year in which Bob Metcalfe said the internet would collapse, we were cruising at around 33.6 kbps, which many considered to be the upper limit of speed available through a standard four-wire phone cable. But it wasn't. The 56 kbps modem was invented in 1996 and became widely available in 1998. Same island, more lichen.

It became increasingly clear that the phone network and the four-wire phone cable weren't cut out for transmitting all this new digital data, and part of the solution ironically stemmed from Bob Metcalfe himself. Metcalfe had invented the idea of the Ethernet (and corresponding hardware) back in the 1970s. Ethernets, with their larger bandwidth connections, quickly became popular in universities and large companies.

Cable broadband internet was introduced in the mid-1990s and became widespread at the turn of the century. Using the existing cable television network and its corresponding coaxial wiring, new cable modems, plus Metcalfe's eight-wire RJ45 Ethernet cords, we were able to radically increase data speeds—from 56 kpbs to between 1000 and 6000 kpbs—or 1 to 6 megabits per second (many cable modems are currently capable of speeds up to 30 mbps, but few internet service providers supported those speeds back then). This was a true bandwidth revolution, and we soon found ourselves with more carrying capacity than we knew what to do with. New island, fresh lichen.

Over time, we invented larger and faster cables—T1, T3, fiber optics. Collectively, we call these larger bandwidth cables "broadband" because they're made up of broader physical bands, wires, and cables than the phone network. In moving from our old phone system infrastructure to a shiny new broadband infrastructure, we essentially moved the internet from one island to a larger island. There was plenty of space to roam and lots of virtual lichen for us to eat. But now we're getting too big even for this island.

IV

In the brain, limitations of skull size and energy consumption are offset by evolutionary innovations. It turns out that the brain is an expensive asset because it consumes so much of the body's energy. In nature, food is often scarce, and hunting for calories is a time-consuming and dangerous task. One of the reasons that animals have relatively small brains is that efficiency trumps intelligence. In fact, humans have evolved cultural and technological tools to offset the energy hogs in our skulls.

If you had to guess what one thing separates us from the rest of the animal kingdom, it would likely come from a predictable list: bipedalism, opposable thumbs, use of fire. These things are important, but Richard Wrangham, a Harvard University anthropologist, put forth a new theory that has recently been supported by research from Suzana Herculano-Houzel, a neuroscientist at the Federal University of Rio de Janeiro in Brazil. They have shown that what sets us apart is our ability to cook. For us to evolve bigger brains than our closest ape cousins, we needed to increase our caloric intake by over 700 calories per day. That may seem easy these days (one Big Mac would do the trick with a few calories to spare), but remember, we started off as raw foodies. That posed a huge problem for our former selves: eating raw food is incredibly time consuming—it takes a gorilla nearly 80 percent of its day to forage and consume the calories needed to maintain a brain one third our size. To grow our brains from ape-sized to human-sized would have required spending well over nine hours crunching veggies and chewing on raw meat each day. That would have left little time for anything else, rendering our larger brains useless.

Cooking food actually changes its composition, which allows cooked food to be consumed more quickly and digested faster. By cooking food, our ancestors consumed many more calories than they would have otherwise, which provided fuel for their hungry growing brains and left them with extra time to use those brains. Herculano-Houzel, after reporting her findings to the National Academy of Sciences, went so far as to say that "the reason we have more neurons than any other animal alive is that cooking allowed this qualitative change." Humans set ourselves apart from other animals because cooking increased our energy intake enough to support a bigger brain.

We once believed that what made us smart was descending from the trees or becoming biped or discovering fire, but perhaps it was our gluttonous consumption. We increased our carrying capacity by creating efficiencies that other animals did not have available. Or as Herculano-Houzel says, "The more I think about it, the more I bow to my kitchen. It's the reason we are here."

V

The internet is also an energy hog; green it is not. We are now beginning to understand the massive energy it will take to sustain the internet's growth. Think of all the things that use energy: cars, factories, drilling, China. None of them individually compares to the consumption growth of the internet, which recent estimates peg at roughly 2 percent of all energy consumed.

As with cooking to increase caloric intake or migrating to find lichen, internet companies across the globe have moved to energy-rich environments. In fact, most internet companies don't actually reside in Silicon Valley; their people may be there, but not their technologies. These companies have moved their systems to areas where energy is abundant. For example, the data centers for Google, Facebook, Netflix, and many other companies are housed near abundant and cheap energy sources. Some sit near water dams, others near wind power, still others near coal, natural gas, or nuclear power.

Google alone uses enough energy each year to power 200,000 homes. That's roughly 260 million watts, or one-quarter of the output of a large nuclear power plant. When you think of the meteoric growth of the internet, you can quickly see that there is an alarming problem ahead of us: the internet is on track to consume 20 percent of the world's power, just as the brain consumes

20 percent of the body's power. At the internet's current rate of growth, it will get there within ten years.

This leads to an obvious problem. If the internet continues along this growth trajectory, it could take down the entire energy grid and either collapse or accelerate global warming to an unsustainable rate in the process. Luckily the internet, like the brain, has evolved a few shortcuts to maximize its energy efficiency. Remember TCP and how the brain, ants, and the internet all use this technology to regulate the flow of information? TCP is basically an efficiency gateway. It actively looks for bottlenecks and frees them by slowing down transmissions. Those slowdowns paradoxically speed up the entire system, thereby creating efficiency and energy savings.

TCP isn't the brain's only trick. Our brains compartmentalize different functions to increase efficiency. Brain scientists call this modularity. We have distinct regions for language, vision, memory, and most other high-level cognitive functions. Speed and efficiency are the hallmarks of a modular system—it is much more economical when many of the areas that control a specific function are close together. Just imagine an airplane with half of the controls in the cockpit and the rest in the rear lavatory, and you'll get the idea.

Modularity has become the norm on the internet. We have structured large parts of the internet into what are called server farms, massive storage facilities housed near one another. Part of the reason for this is power constraints, but it is also an efficiency trick. Huge speed efficiencies result from having Facebook, Netflix, Amazon, and all of the smaller guys sharing space. It turns out that much of the internet is housed in large buildings known as "carrier hotels." One carrier hotel in New York City has over one million square feet more than the Empire State Building. In a crowded city, it contains mostly computers and wires. Imagine the value of that building. Actually, you don't have to imagine: Google bought it for $1.9 billion in the highest priced real estate transaction recorded across the globe in 2010. This particular piece of real estate was purchased for Google's most valuable asset, which is not human capital, but computers and wires. And even though Google owns the building, the real estate continues to be shared with some of the largest—and smallest—names across the internet, creating a virtuous cycle of increased efficiency.

The human brain's capacity for reason, consciousness, judgment, and decision making is due in large part to a module called the cerebral cortex, a region that is larger as a percentage of our brains than it is in any other animal. Elephants may have bigger brains overall, but our relative cortical size is much larger. Invertebrates don't have cortexes at all. The newest part of the cerebral cortex, the neocortex, evolved in humans only 200,000 years ago. It is responsible for virtually all areas of higher reasoning.

Cloud computing is modularity at its finest, and it may evolve into the cerebral cortex of the internet. Most people think of cloud computing as a way to store information, which it is, but clouds do more than that. Computing clouds allow for independent computations to happen across the internet, giving individuals access to virtually unlimited computing resources. Where you were once limited to your own computers or servers to process information, the cloud allows you to tap the resources of universities, governments, and large companies such as Amazon, Google, IBM, and Microsoft.

There is incredible efficiency associated with this model, as large entities can rent out idle computing resources at a fraction of the cost. But much more is going on behind the scenes. Clouds allow you to tie many small computers together to make large distributed supercomputers. Google's cloud, for instance, is composed of nothing more than a bunch of inexpensive desktop PCs. But when you put together hundreds of millions of those desktops, the computational power is awesome, more powerful than any machine on earth (including biological machines like our own brains). Because the individual units are independent of one another, computations can happen in parallel, just as in the brain. Individual computers can't do that; clouds make it happen. Parallel processing—where multiple things happen at once—has been linked directly to consciousness and self-awareness. It is here where real intelligence, and possibly even consciousness, will likely come online.

The human brain has an incredibly efficient memory system, which is actually divided into two distinct systems. The first stores information permanently in the brain, which creates our long-term memories. The second is a fleeting memory system that remembers a small amount of information for a small amount of time. The reason for this is efficiency: pulling information from long-term memory is very costly in terms of energy. Short-term memory, on the other hand, is fluid and easily accessible; it's an ideal repository for information the brain is likely to need in the near future. The downside is how small the memory system is—it turns out that our brains can hold only about seven pieces of short-term information at any given time. So short-term memory is quite limited, but that's precisely why it's so efficient.

Mimicking the brain's short-term memory, scientists at MIT invented content delivery networks, or CDNs, in the late 1990s. Since then, companies like Akamai and Edgecast have commercialized variations of the technology. Basically, this technology replicates what the brain does: it creates short-term storage for information that is used often. These companies have built servers all over the world whose purpose is to store information close to where you are. If you are in Singapore trying to reach Facebook or YouTube, you are likely going to see a copy of those pages that come from a server in Singapore hosted by Akamai or Edgecast. Just imagine the amount of time and energy saved by having that information close to home instead of going across the globe to retrieve it. Not surprisingly, this is big business, as nearly 45 percent of all internet traffic flows through a content delivery network.

Myelin sheaths are another interesting innovation, one that has evolved only in vertebrate brains. Myelin is a fatty tissue that wraps the connections going from neuron to neuron. This wrapper acts as insulation, helping the neuron retain information. The advantage of this, again, is speed and efficiency. Without myelin, the information traveling between neurons would decay faster or require more energy to make the trip. In that case, the brain would be smaller and slower; or, at a minimum, the neurons would need to be closer together. If neurons had to be close together to communicate, long spinal cords would be ineffective and would not allow for the simultaneous growth of intelligence and body size, the latter of which is necessary to consume energy to support the former. This is a key reason that vertebrates have larger brains (and vertebrae, for that matter).

Samuel Morse and Alexander Graham Bell both used non-insulated copper wires in early versions of the telegraph and telephone. These lines worked reasonably well over short distances, but the communication decayed over long distances. So they added a synthetic version of myelin—a plastic coating to wrap around the copper. This insulation kept the electrical signal from decaying or completely falling off the copper. We now have all kinds of insulators, from metal and glass to plastic and ceramic.

Each provides added levels of efficiency, reducing the need for energy. This is true with copper, aluminum, and even silicon.

We are not perfect computers; our brains tend to fumble in the dark and make educated guesses. Imagine trying to calculate the trajectory of a flying object as well as its shape, distance, wind velocity, and speed. Computers can do this perfectly, without breaking a sweat. Now imagine lifting your arm and catching a ball—ah, easy. Computers compute; we guess. In that way, our brains are designed to be prediction engines, fallible and full of mistakes, and to these characteristics we owe our baseball prowess. Our brains make guesses and are often wrong. But being wrong can be a good thing: when a system is free to make mistakes, it can offset energy needs with the exorbitant cost of perfection. The brain's lack of perfection saves significant energy without reducing overall intelligence. The brain can do all that fancy ball handling with less energy than is consumed by a single 20-watt light bulb.

The brain's lack of perfection starts from the bottom, with the smallest brain component—the neuron. Neurons aren't just fallible, they are downright faulty: neurons fail to fire when they should between 30 and 90 percent of the time. Our 100 billion neurons fire often enough that misfires do no real harm because the network has enough neurons to correct itself. So even at the neuronal level, the brain prefers expediency to perfection.

Researchers at Stanford and Caltech are currently looking at ways to replicate that error rate in transistors with the hope of reducing energy consumption without compromising performance. They have created the Neurogrid chip, which uses roughly 1/10,000th of the power of a traditional silicon chip. Like neurons, these chips are not perfect, and as a result they require millions of transistors to do the calculating work of just a few traditional ones. But that isn't the point, of course. Ultimately, we are trying to catch the ball, not calculate its trajectory. IBM recently attempted to simulate the brain functionality of 55 million neurons using traditional chips. They did so successfully, but at the cost of 320,000 watts of energy. Like the brain, the Neurogrid chip could perform similarly with less than a watt.

Ultimately, the internet will need to evolve into using different energy sources. The internet is slow and inefficient compared to the way the brain processes information, primarily because the brain's communication system uses chemical and electrical currents whereas the internet currently uses electricity alone. At some point, we will likely create a chemical system to increase the amount of information that can move across the internet. That insight will probably come from research on the chemical communications of the brain, or perhaps even from research on ant communication.

VI

The internet continues to evolve, grow, and increase its overall carrying capacity, but eventually we will run out of virtual lichen on our island. When that happens, it will not necessarily be a bad thing. Just as the brain gains intelligence as it overshoots and collapses, so too may the internet. The brain can be our guide to the internet because the two are so similar. We have substituted hardware for wetware, but the fundamental structures are the same: they are both complex networks capable of calculating, remembering, and communicating. Carrying capacity is never infinite, so we will eventually hit a breakpoint. But when that happens, the results will be exciting to see and will likely yield a smaller, yet more efficient, nimble, and—dare I say it—intelligent internet.

FOUR

SLAVES | NEURONS | THE WEB

F or all their simplicity, neurons do some pretty amazing things. They are autonomous cells that aren't physically connected, yet they communicate with one another. They are plastic, in the sense that they are able to switch tasks when called upon. The same neurons can be used for language, hearing, decision making, and virtually every other function in the brain. It is the humble neuron that allows us to think and act.

Despite that remarkable power, neurons are largely listless. Neurons turn on and off, nothing more. They aren't aggressive, they don't fight to survive, and they generally perform the same task over and over. They are selfless; their goals and objectives are that of the larger whole. Neurons act as a network, not as individuals.

The modest ant does some amazing things as well. Ants defend their territories against predators; they form complex social structures; they use tools and create meals from non-food substances. One species even invented air-conditioning for their nest, based on a system of pushing out warm air and pulling in fresh air, millions of years before we humans thought of it.

Unlike neurons, ants are not inert. Some ants are downright aggressive, going to surprising lengths to claw themselves to the top of the heap. There is one group that is especially so—the roughly 100 species of ants collectively known as slave-making ants.

Slave-making ants don't clean house, cook food, or take care of their babies. They actually don't even *know how* to do any of those things. They're pretty much good at only one thing: finding others to do their work. Slave-makers raid the nests of other ant colonies and steal all their eggs. Those ants grow up as slaves, and they do pretty much everything for their masters: groom them, feed them, defend them from bigger insects, you name it. If the colony moves to a new nest, the slaves will even carry their masters to their new abode.

In ethical terms, stealing babies and making them into slaves is pretty bad. But murder is even worse. In order to steal the eggs of another colony, the slave-makers must first go to war—these prodigious ants ruthlessly kill any ant that gets in the way. Opportunistic slave-maker queens follow these raiders into a colony and take advantage of the chaos created by the raid. The young aspiring queen slips into the nest, finds the queen ant, and literally chokes her to death. Then she eats the old queen so that she smells like the queen's pheromones. The rest of the ants never know the difference, giving the young slave-maker queen an instant colony of her own.

The peaceful, simple neuron has no direct parallel to a slave-making ant. But within the brain is another novelty that is very much a slave-maker: the idea. Ideas sit on top of neurons, riding them in much the way that slave-makers ride their slaves. But more than that, ideas propagate: they jump from brain to brain as they spread with a fervor no less intense than that of slave-maker ants attacking a colony.

Ideas can be good or bad. Some, like the cure for polio, are positive; others, like fascism, have evil consequences. But ideas tend to spread and infect the minds of others. In many ways, they are like diseases in that they enter our minds without warning and cannot be stopped. If an idea is contagious, it is committed to memory and spread to others; otherwise, it is relegated to the periphery of our unconscious. Ideas are more powerful than any physical force: they alter people's minds, making them do things they wouldn't otherwise do. In this way, ideas, perhaps even more than actions, change the course of history.

I

Slave-making ants are the Napoleons of the ant kingdom. For these mini-conquistadors, it seems that the sky's the limit. So what's stopping them from uniting all ants into a massive super-colony and taking over the world?

It is a pretty frightening thought given the sheer number of ants on the planet. There are more ants than mammals; most chillingly, the total weight of all the ants on earth exceeds that of humans. If ants could organize themselves into a supercolony, they could conceivably be the most powerful species alive.

Fortunately for us, ant colonies are networks; they only grow until they reach a breakpoint. Once they've reached that point, even slave-makers stop raiding to grow their ranks. As we've seen, carrying capacity is non-negotiable.

The carrying capacity of an ant colony is bound by physical factors including the abundance of food and the availability of materials to build nests. But some ant colonies, such as Deborah Gordon's harvester ants, have plenty of both. They live underground in vast wastelands—they could conceivably expand their nests exponentially. There are hundreds of colonies in a small area, so clearly there is plenty of food and water. So why do harvester ant colonies top off at around 10,000 ants and maintain that population for years? Why don't slave-making ants just steal the carrying capacity of another colony and thus increase their capacity?

It turns out that physical capacity is a necessary condition for a network, but it is not sufficient by itself. The carrying capacity of a network is limited not just by physical size but also by *utility*. Each ant colony reaches a certain population that maximizes its ability to meet its goals: find food, remain healthy, and reproduce. Above that breakpoint, there is no additional value for adding more ants to the colony.

Not only is there no additional value, but adding more ants is counterproductive. Ants communicate mainly through scents. If you've ever tried to cover a bad odor with a combination of bleach, 409, and Febreze, you know that piling too many scents on top of each other is a bad thing.

Remember, ants respond to patterns of interactions. Deborah Gordon played a critical role in this discovery, and she explains it this way: "An ant uses its recent experience of interactions to decide what to do. The pattern of interaction itself, rather than any signal transferred, acts as the message. What matters is not what one ant tells another when they meet, but simply *that* they meet. An ant operates according to a rule such as, 'If I meet another ant with odor A about three times in the next 30 seconds, I will go out to forage; if not, I will stay here.'" Ants are not the best at counting and have short memories, so you can imagine that too many ants make it simply too distracting for an individual ant to focus on the task at hand. Instead of growing in numbers, it makes more sense for a mature colony to form a stable population.

II

The important thing to remember about carrying capacity is that just as a network can be made of neurons, ants, or computers, carrying capacity can differ as well. We have seen how energy is a critical factor in the carrying capacity for most hardware and biological networks. That is because physical stuff requires energy. The brain, being a physical network, is a big energy hog, which is why we see many animals consumed by the task of energy consumption.

When software systems are built on physical networks, their carrying capacity depends not only upon energy but also upon utility. Survival for this type of network means staying useful and relevant.

Think of how an idea remains top of mind: through memory. Memories are the software layer of the brain. The brain's networks of neurons form a semantic network of memories, which carry ideas. In theory, we could hold an unlimited number of ideas in our heads, but our brains would become quite cluttered. Consider Jill Price, a woman who can remember every single day of her life since she was 11 years old. "Starting on February 5th, 1980, I remember everything. That was a Tuesday." Price remembers literally everything, even random news events that aren't directly relevant but that happened during her lifetime. Ask Price about Bing Crosby's death, and she'll respond, "Oh yes, he died on a golf course in Spain," and proceed to give you the time of death and other arbitrary details. Price has perfect memory, what in clinical terms is called hyperthymesia.

There are only about a dozen documented (i.e., real) cases of hyperthymesia. There are no tricks, gimmicks, or strategies to these perfect memories. This condition is also not like autism or savant syndrome; hyperthymesiacs are otherwise normal. Given that, it seems pretty powerful to have a perfect memory. So why haven't we evolved as a species to remember everything if our brains have the capacity to handle it? It turns out that human memory has a breakpoint as well. Too much of a good thing, it seems, isn't so good.

Price has battled with depression, anxiety, and migraines, the latter of which required her to take five aspirins a day starting in early childhood. Price describes her experience as "nonstop, uncontrollable and exhausting . . . I run my entire life through my head every day, and it drives me crazy." One would think that surely a perfect memory has an upside, possibly in learning. Not for Price and other hyperthymesiacs. Despite her "gift," Price performed unremarkably in school, often earning Bs, Cs, and Ds. "I had to study hard. I'm not a genius," she explains.

Worse yet, hyperthymesic memory often gets in the way of other higher level functions, such as decision making. This makes sense: if we all had perfect memories, we would likely be very slow to remember, process information, and make decisions. Too much information would clog our brains and make it hard to sift the dirt from the gold. There is a reason our brains discard most information they process and only keep that which is most useful. Irrelevant ideas need to die, just like irrelevant neurons.

The theme at this point should be clear. All hardware networks grow only to the extent that there is physical carrying capacity—energy—available. This is true for ants, deer, neurons, and the internet. Software resides on hardware, so it is naturally bound by the hardware's capacity. But in addition to physical carrying capacity, software networks must also yield to a utility breakpoint. For memories and ideas, going beyond that breakpoint is really bad.

III

On the internet, websites are the parallel to memories. Websites are the software of the internet, just as memories are the software of the mind. While the key to the survival of the internet is its physical carrying capacity (i.e., the size and energy consumption of its tubes, wires, processors, switches, and routers), the World Wide Web is something different. It is the usable layer of the internet—the websites and programs that allow us to communicate, store memory, and transmit ideas over the physical internet.

When the World Wide Web was invented in 1993, it changed the internet overnight. Prior to that, the internet was a cool idea; with the web, it became an indispensable phenomenon. The World Wide Web is home to websites that carry ideas—they store, transport, and propagate them in a way that was never possible before. A single website can hold infinite information, instantly accessible to the world's population. Websites transformed the internet from lackluster to blockbuster.

The web, along with the ideas it spreads, has grown enormously. There were no websites in 1993, 20 million websites in 2002, and 600 million sites by 2012. This is an astounding growth number: a person growing that large from birth would be able to touch the moon by the time he was ten. In fact, we've had to add new words to our vocabulary to describe the size of the web. Computers first held megabytes, then gigabytes, and we struggled to grasp the sheer magnitude of those numbers. The web is now described in petabytes and exabytes. But even those numbers are too small, as it is predicted that the web will grow to a couple of zettabytes (10^{21} bytes) by 2016.

Zettabyte? Just how big is a zettabyte? It's the equivalent of all the information contained in every movie ever made traveling across the internet every three minutes for an entire year. The web, just like a mind, is a slave to the huge quantities of ideas it shares every day.

Because it is software, the web isn't limited by any physical size maximums. But just because the web *can* hold an infinite number of websites doesn't mean that it has infinite carrying capacity. The web is more than just a big collection of websites with individual addresses. The web is so named because it's a network, like a spider's web. As such, it is subject to the limits of carrying capacity. Much more important than the sheer number of websites is the amount of useful and accessible information.

Clearly, we find the web useful. Each of us views an estimated 2,600 webpages across almost 90 unique sites per month. We spent an average of 70 minutes a day on the web in 2012, up from only 46 minutes in 2002. When you consider that we're also surfing, sending, and downloading at lightning fast speeds compared to ten years ago, it's clear that we're getting more out of the web than ever before. But it's getting noisy and congested, and some would say there are simply too many ants.

IV

Over the past few years I've had an uncomfortable sense that someone, or something, has been tinkering with my brain, remapping the neural circuitry, reprogramming the memory. My mind isn't going—so far as I can tell—but it's changing. I'm not thinking the way I used to think . . . what the Net seems to be doing is chipping away my capacity for concentration and contemplation. My mind now expects to take in information the way the Net distributes it: in a swiftly moving stream of particles. Once I was a scuba diver in the sea of words. Now I zip along the surface like a guy on a Jet Ski.

Thus begins Nicholas Carr's widely circulated 2008 article in *The Atlantic,* "Is Google Making Us Stupid?" (Carr expanded his point in his bestselling and Pulitzer Prize–nominated book, *The Shallows: What the Internet Is Doing to Our Brains.*) Carr isn't alone. His contemporaries, including Larry Rosen (*iDisorder: Understanding Our Obsession with Technology and Overcoming Its Hold on Us*) and Daniel Sieberg (*The Digital Diet: The 4-Step Plan to Break Your Tech Addiction and Regain Balance in Your Life*), agree that our dependence on the web is dangerous and that it's changing us for the worse. Their colleague Dr. Kimberly Young (author of both *Caught in the Net* and *Tangled in the Web*) runs the Center for Internet Addiction to help the afflicted recognize and treat their high-tech dependencies. This is now a serious problem, with the American Psychological Association in 2013 classifying "Internet-use disorder" as a condition "recommended for further study," coinciding with a 16-year-old girl making headlines for drugging her parents with sleeping pills in order to use the internet past her curfew.

I'm not convinced that the web is damaging our brains, but it's clearly a messy place. The web browser has become the Swiss Army knife of tools—it easily takes the place of an encyclopedia, a stack of newspapers, the dictionary, the thesaurus, the calculator, the clock, the television, and the shopping mall.

The world at our fingertips clearly comes with a price. It's hard to use the web for even the most basic task without being distracted by links, ads, emails, tweets, alerts, and headlines. The ones we vilify and avoid are the ones there to sell us something, but even the good diversions diffuse our attention and concentration. These distractions reduce the usefulness of the web.

V

The value of the web has been questioned before. Almost from its infancy, the web was too big for us to wrap our heads around. During the first ten years, we massively exceeded the carrying capacity, and the usefulness dropped significantly. People just weren't finding what they needed. Google and other search engines were created to act as gateways, shrinking down the web to a manageable size. The engines drastically increased the utility of the web by pointing us toward what they consider to be the most valuable sites and allowing us to completely ignore the rest. And still, as *USA Today* reported in 2007, "the Web is just too big for any current organization scheme to handle."

Despite the help from search engines, the World Wide Web has exceeded its breakpoint. The quantity of information available is higher than the carrying capacity or usefulness. The web continues to grow, but its utility is falling. It's a classic case of too much of a good thing, like Price's memory, and the whole network is set to collapse if we don't cull it down.

Signs of the web's breakpoint have been around for a few years. The most significant, though rarely reported, sign is that the growth of the web is actually slowing down. While growth in the number of websites was over 800 percent in the first ten years, it slowed to a paltry 19 percent in 2012 and is projected to be less than that for the next five years. The number of users is also declining; there were 4 percent fewer people using the web on their

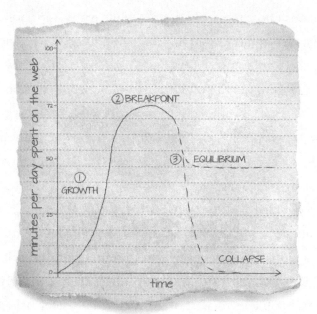

Image 4.1: Will the Web Collapse?

PCs in 2012 than the year before. In addition, the amount of time people are spending on the web is dropping: from 72 minutes per day in 2011 to 70 minutes in 2012. This is a small change, but the trend will continue.

For the web, collapse won't be as spectacular as the mass extinction of reindeer on St. Matthew Island or cannibalism on Easter Island. Collapse on the web means that we simply won't use it anymore. We're already seeing signs of this, in large part as a result of the rise of mobile applications, or apps. If the World Wide Web is a Swiss Army knife, an app is the fish hook disgorger or a wood chisel. It performs one specific task. There's no temptation to unnecessarily fiddle with the scissors or the can opener because those are completely different apps that you must make a conscious effort to use. Note that while many apps pull content from the web and reformat it (*The Economist* or Yelp), most apps bypass the web completely (Taxi Magic or Uber). They use the internet to connect to content servers, but they do not actually download from, or upload to, the World Wide Web. The distinction isn't always obvious, but apps are fundamentally different from the web, and apps are taking from the web an increasingly larger share of the internet's growth.

The average iPhone owner already has 108 apps and spent 127 minutes a day using them in 2012 (up from 94 minutes in 2011); numbers for Android users are comparable. That is already almost double the time the average person currently spends on the web. Of course, part of the reason we're increasingly using apps instead of the web is that we're mobile, but that's only part of the story, as anyone who prefers to use their iPad rather than their laptop knows. A weather app is not only more convenient than watching the evening news, it's also more convenient than going to weather.com.

Imagine if you had to choose between giving up your apps or your browser on your mobile phone or tablet. That is a no-brainer for me: I'd ditch the browser, which I tend to use no more than any other app. Definitely when I'm on the go, and often when I'm just hanging out at home, my personal collection of apps is far more useful to me than the web. As tablets replace computers, the web will be relegated to a position no higher than that of a "super app."

The rise of mobile isn't doing the web any favors, and by all accounts, mobile is skyrocketing. It more than doubled in 2011 for the fourth year in a row. Cisco predicts that mobile traffic will increase by a factor of 18 in the next five years. That growth will come at the expense of the web. It should be noted that this doesn't necessarily mean that all that traffic will be apps; smart-phones and tablets come equipped with web browsers, and almost all major websites (and many smaller ones) offer mobile versions of their content. Mobile versions are often simpler, pared down, and curated versions of the real thing—just like an app.

When you click on the tech category on CNN using a mobile browser, you're presented with a half dozen of the most popular CNN technology stories of the day. After you get to the bottom of one story, you'll see another half dozen links to similar stories at the bottom of the page (if you use the CNN app, your only choice is to go back—there are no additional links at the end of each story). By contrast, if you read the same story on the regular CNN site, you'll find about 30 links to other articles, a dozen sponsored ads, and a full navigation bar that will help you find even more content. It's tough to properly surf on a phone browser, and that's a problem for a network that depends upon its users' gliding from link to link.

Clearly, mobile sites must be small in order to accommodate the small physical size of a mobile phone. But that's only part of the story. Mobile sites are small because there is now more value, more utility, in offering less. The web has hit its breakpoint un-der the weight of having too much of a good thing. The newer, more nimble mobile net is cutting through the clutter in the same way that search engines cut through the clutter of the early World Wide Web.

VI

For all of its weaknesses, the web is still pretty awesome. But it must collapse somewhat to find equilibrium. It must become smarter, denser, more relevant. But how? We need look no further than the brain for a roadmap. Both on the web and in the brain, links are key. And not just the number of links, but also the depth and dimensionality of those links. If we can mimic the structure of the brain on the web, we can make it more meaningful and, ultimately, more useful.

Links are vital to the survival of a network, and the web is already sparse in these terms. Each website is connected to an average of 60 other websites. By contrast, each neuron in the brain links to thousands of other neurons in a tightly connected fashion. If certain neuronal links aren't used regularly, the links disappear and the neuron dies. Not so with the web, and that's part of the reason it is cluttered with things we don't need.

The brain has two types of links: inbound (axons) and outbound (dendrites), and sometimes two neurons are connected by both an inbound and an outbound link. Two-way links are obviously more meaningful than one-way links. The brain's software networks have similar connections. Language, for instance, is stored in memory by linking relevant information with either one-way or two-way links. The idea that a Toyota is a car creates a one-way relationship in our minds because all Toyotas are cars but not all cars are Toyotas. The idea that a car is an auto creates a two-way relationship because cars and autos are synonymous. Information is retrieved in the brain by traversing these links in a manner in which one memory activates another until the right information is located.

Adding this layer of meaning to the web will require a change in its underlying structure, but it's not technically difficult. Currently, links are royal blue, indicating a connection from one page to another. It wouldn't be hard to show a two-way link in a different color, or perhaps a different font size. The power of this minor change in structure would be immense: it would immediately give users the ability to know just how strong a link is across two websites or just how close a relationship is between two pieces of information.

Think about it this way—if Joe's Plumbing site is linked to the *New York Times,* that link is probably far more relevant if the *New York Times* also links to Joe's Plumbing. In the latter case, it's less likely that Joe's Plumbing is trying to artificially strengthen its position by linking to the authority of the *New York Times.* In the social world, it's like following someone on Twitter. I can follow Natalie Portman if I want to, and that link has some value, but not nearly as much as if Natalie (please) follows me as well. When it's a two-way link, there's more meaning. It's an intimate connection, an actual relationship.

Neurons also have weight to their links. In other words, there are different values to thoughts and their relationship to other thoughts. This is reflected in the relative strengths of habits and memories. There isn't a similar link-weighting system currently on the web, but there's no reason we can't eventually build this facet into the web's very fabric.

What dimensions should we consider for link weighting? Relevance, usefulness, significance, and prominence are some of the characteristics that should factor in. Besides whether a link is one-way or two-way, the relevance and importance of a link need to be demarcated. Again, it could be a color code, where blue might represent the best links on the page, green second best, yellow third, red fourth, and so on until a link is rendered irrelevant and automatically removed.

In the beginning, site owners may choose their most important links, but ultimately the web should be allowed to evolve through natural selection. The web could integrate how many people click on a link, how much time is spent on that page, and whether users eventually return to the original site. It could consider a user's demographics and history to make a personalized prediction of link relevance. For example, perhaps links to locations geographically close to a user should be weighted more heavily. Past history could also play a role: if a user has clicked on a link before, or if he has spent time on other sites that also connect to the link, those are important factors. Taken together, all of this data could allow for dynamic link-weighting based on relevance and utility.

All of these innovations would make the web more meaningful, but the ultimate feat would be to also make it smaller. To do this, we could allow links to automatically fade and ultimately disappear if they aren't used after a period of time. This could be true of unused websites as well. This is directly analogous to the brain's process in which irrelevant neurons selflessly commit cellular suicide. We need websites to do the same. It's what makes us smart, and it's what will make the web smart.

Of course, much of this may be untenable, as websites are governed by companies, not nature. The greater good is not always a primary business concern. But we can still, at a minimum, quarantine or mark as offensive those websites that make up the clutter of the web, at least until they prove to do more good than harm.

VII

The web will continue to be useful despite having hit a breakpoint. Our goal now should be to shepherd it toward equilibrium so that it doesn't implode. We must make it less distracting and more meaningful, but I personally don't subscribe to the theory that it's hurting our brains.

Every new technology has its cynics. When Gutenberg invented the printing press in the fifteenth century, many believed that mass printing would alter our brains. Rumor has it that the great Socrates was against the written word itself. Many warned how the telegraph, telephone, radio, movies, and—of course—television would rot our brains.

The journal *Nature* published an article in 1889 titled "Nature's Revenge on Genius," arguing that each new technological invention causes us to grow increasingly dim. A predecessor to Nicholas Carr, the author cited a newfangled technology called electricity as public enemy number one. It is worth reading a few sentences to see just how much fear surrounded something so commonplace to us today, and how similar it seems to the way some people describe the web now:

> At present our most dangerous pet is electricity—in the telegraph, the street lamp and the telephone. We have introduced electric power into our simplest domestic industries, and we have woven this most subtile of agents, once active only in the sublimest manifestations of Omnipotence, like a web about our dwellings, and filled our atmosphere with the filaments of death . . . It is urged that electric lighting is not essential to the public comfort. It is not a necessity but a luxury. By abolishing it we reduce our danger appreciably . . . The telephone is the most dangerous of all because it enters into every dwelling. Its interminable network of wires is a perpetual menace to life and property.

Atomic bombs aside, history has generally shown that new technologies end up enabling us, not encasing us in "a web about our dwellings." The medium is never the issue, though the content occasionally can be. The web itself isn't broken; it's up to us to separate the bad from the good in order to make it even better.

FIVE

BREAD | MOBILE | SOCIAL

After the fall of the Soviet Union, an economist in London received a question from a colleague in Saint Petersburg, Russia: "Who is in charge of the supply of bread to the population of London?" As someone living in a democratic country, it is almost impossible to understand that question. To say it sounds strange understates the point. But the British economist bit his lip and gave a serious reply: What do you mean, who's in charge—"nobody is in charge."

Accustomed to an environment in which every detail of life was centrally planned, officials in the newly capitalist Russia found it unbelievable that such a thriving supply-chain network could be self-organized. When you think about it, it is truly incredible and counterintuitive that elaborate tasks can be accomplished without anyone in charge.

But that's the way free markets work: they thrive by having limited central command, limited bureaucracy, limited regulation. In a free market, networks of companies seamlessly provide services that rely on complex chains of events. For something as simple as bread, there are dough manufacturers, bakers, storefronts, and a host of other businesses that must work seamlessly without central leadership to deliver a product to consumers. Even the British economist, after thinking about the question, retreated from the obviousness of his answer: "the answer, when one thinks carefully about it, is astonishingly hard to believe."

Perhaps this is why it took scientists until the twentieth century to figure out that the brain has no central command, and that neither the queen nor any other ant directs the colony. Perhaps the US government understood this when it relinquished control of the internet in 1995. Perhaps it was also clear to the European Organization for Nuclear Research (CERN), where the World Wide Web was created, when they wisely announced in 1993 that the web would be free for anyone to use.

So all of our favorite networks—the brain, ant colonies, the internet, and the web—organize themselves. Just like London's network of wheat growers, bakers, and grocery stores, which ensure that any Brit with a few pounds can buy a loaf of bread, *no one is in charge.*

|

Having no one in charge is great for bread distribution, great for Mother Nature, even great for the internet. But companies need to have someone in charge. Companies are more like dictatorships than democracies, and this is generally a good thing. Top-down leadership tends to work for businesses in general, as centralized decision making is often critical to success. But when a business is running a network, central command is no better than the results that we saw in Russia before the fall of Communism: long bread lines and systemic failures that led to collapse. Businesses are focused on growth and profitability, which is often at odds with efficiency and stability. Inevitably, business leaders will push a network beyond its breakpoint and just keep on pushing.

It is ironic that one of the first people to be in charge of a major social network was Tom Anderson. As a high school freshman in 1985, he figured out how to hack into the computing system of Chase Manhattan Bank, which should have been impenetrable to a high school kid. Anderson shared his newfound knowledge with his friends, ultimately prompting a major FBI raid in which agents confiscated the computers of Anderson and 24 of his buddies, thereby shutting down the hacking scheme.

The loss of his beloved computer didn't slow Anderson down, and after working at several successful technology companies, he cofounded MySpace in 2003. Anderson and his team propelled the network into hypergrowth, leading it from a handful of users to several hundred million accounts by 2006, the same year it became the most visited website on earth, with more monthly visitors than Google.

Back in 2007, I wrote a prediction for my book *Wired for Thought* that MySpace would soon be overtaken by a lesser-known network called Facebook. Most people, including my Harvard Press editors, thought I was delusional. MySpace was all the rage, and experts were predicting it would overtake Google, Yahoo!, the written word, even communication itself. But just like every social network before it, MySpace flamed out.

Fast forward to the writing of this book in 2012, and it's Facebook's turn. By the time this book is edited, published, distributed, and in your hands, we will have some irrefutable stats about Facebook's usage decline. This is a company that went public in May 2012 at $38 per share and was trading at less than $19 two months later. Why the huge drop? Pundits suggested many reasons, including poor investor relations, lack of revenue, and expiring lockups. Others repeated far too often that perhaps CEO Mark Zuckerberg was "in over his hoodie." Now this is a guy who is a revered prodigy, who built Facebook from the ground up. (Criminal record aside, MySpace's Tom Anderson was no slouch himself.)

Despite his intelligence, Zuckerberg may in fact be part of the problem. Facebook, like all social networks before it, is a man-made network controlled by one company, and that company is controlled by one man. It could be argued that it wasn't created with the explicit goal of making money, but it is a company with stakeholders and—as of 2012—public shareholders. Growth and profitability are necessary to the survival of the company, but that could mean the demise of the network itself.

When networks are free to grow unencumbered, like bread distribution or the internet, they naturally hit a point of equilibrium. That is why they work: efficient networks yield to the environment's limits. But when a network is run for profit, it is only natural to want to push beyond the breakpoint. The danger is that unnatural, forced growth can cause a network to collapse. This is what happened to MySpace, and it is now happening to Facebook.

This situation begs several questions. Is it possible to balance the needs of a for-profit company with the natural network stages of growth, breakpoint, and equilibrium? Is it possible for someone to be in charge of such a network, or does centralized control automatically kill it? Is it inevitable that controlled networks will collapse, or can the smartest among us, the Zuckerbergs of the world, shepherd them through their natural stages and help the networks reach intelligent equilibriums?

II

Clearly, central command hasn't limited the first stage of networks, exponential growth. We've witnessed the incredible growth of social network after social network. Not just Facebook and MySpace, but also Classmates.com and Friendster. Each in their time looked as if they could grow forever. But in the case of Classmates.com, Friendster, and MySpace, each imploded after hitting its breakpoint.

Like all software, social networks are limited in terms of their ability to engage and satisfy their users: their survival depends upon their usefulness. Users hope to accomplish specific tasks when they log on to a social network to, well . . . socialize. Having too few users creates an obvious problem: there aren't enough people to interact with. The growth phase is necessary to build critical mass, and for every MySpace there are at least a dozen other networks that never got remotely close to the right size.

But a network of too many individuals can also create trouble. An intimate cocktail party is terribly boring if there are only two people, but it becomes overwhelming with two thousand. In the latter case, the party becomes crowded, cluttered, and utterly impractical.

How much socializing are we capable of? For insight, we can again turn to the brain—specifically, the concept of neocortical processing (brain math). British anthropologist Robin Dunbar theorized that neocortical processing limits the number of meaningful social relationships a person can maintain. For humans, that number is estimated to be somewhere around 150. This means that it is difficult for you to maintain more than 150 relationships—that's the social breakpoint of the brain. In theory, any network dependent on the social capacity of the human mind would share that limit. Interestingly, the creators of a social networking site called Path, launched in 2010, were inspired by what is now known as "Dunbar's Number." Path allows its users to connect to a maximum of 150 friends.

But Facebook is already well beyond that point. The average Facebook user has 262 "friends" on the site, so it stands to reason that a significant portion of these friends are not high quality. What's the result? Getting a notification that April Ridmoore downloaded *"Call Me Maybe"* on Spotify. Who's April? Some girl who went out with your younger brother in high school and "poked" you last year.

Facebook has tried, in some ways, to restrict the unfettered growth of its network. They make it easy to turn off notifications, and have made great strides in putting the kibosh on as many of these as possible. And the "random" people you encounter on Facebook are generally people you know, people you used to know, or people only one degree of separation from you (unlike MySpace, in which users often received dozens of completely random friend requests per week).

Essentially, Facebook is a "network of networks," making it a smarter and more successful social network than its predecessors. As the company notes, "Facebook is made up of many networks, each based around a workplace, region, high school or college." Each of these networks is tightly connected in the sense that each has many users who have strong connections to one another. Across those networks, however, the user relationships are sparser (just as the brain's neurons link mostly to those neurons within their sub-networks). This arrangement started in a controlled way for Facebook—first with Harvard, then to other schools, and finally to corporations. This network of networks approach is what led me to predict in 2007 that Facebook would overtake MySpace, which had no such tight-knit clusters.

But it only takes a few unsolicited, valueless notifications, and the utility of Facebook goes down for its users. It is simply inefficient to spend any of your precious neocortical processing capacity finding out about the lives of people who are irrelevant to you—people who will never be one of your 150 meaningful social relationships—even if they are friends of friends.

So what do you do, as a user, when you find yourself in a network that is too large? One might think the logical thing would be to cull your friends list, unsubscribe from updates, and block all notifications. But few people do this. Instead, individuals decrease their usage and delete their accounts, ultimately looking for the next new network to hitch on to, one with a cleaner, less distracting social structure. Having reached a breakpoint by exceeding its capacity to be useful, the old network, like all social networks before it, dies.

But remember that there is an alternative. We've seen that the best way to increase the carrying capacity of the web is to make it more useful and less distracting. Such is also the case with social networks. Again, we can look to the brain as an example. After it reaches breakpoint, the brain filters out extraneous information through cellular suicide. It also deepens the important connections. In turn, we become wiser.

What if Facebook could become wiser? Separate out the fluff and strengthen the important relationships along the lines of the brain. Eliminate weak links and automatically delete friendships that aren't active. Make it more difficult to request a friend who doesn't share mutual friends. Bring activity related to a user's strongest relationships to the forefront and allow the weakest to fade away. Facebook must help its users to efficiently nurture and groom their packs of 150, their "real" social networks, while filtering everything not directly relevant. The company has made some strides on this score, but they must redouble their efforts. It is Facebook's only chance at increasing value.

Interestingly, this back-to-basics approach has been tried accidentally with great success. The mobile browser and the app versions of Facebook are pared-down versions of the website. Everything is stripped out except for the basics: posting to a wall, reading news feeds, sending and receiving messages. In other words, communicating with the people most important to you. Of course, it wasn't Facebook's intention to reduce distractions; these changes were born out of necessity. Mobile devices are just too small to have extraneous information.

The results, nonetheless, are striking. In 2012, Facebook users spent about seven hours per month on the mobile versions of Facebook versus only six hours on their computers. Nielsen reported that, for the first time ever, Facebook had fewer unique PC users in 2012 than in the previous year. However, the mobile versions continued to demonstrate record growth. Facebook on the web is already beyond its breakpoint and declining. But on mobile devices, it is showing healthy record growth. It turns out that, paradoxically, less stuff equals more usage.

To be sure, a big part of the reason for mobile growth is simply that users are more likely to have their smartphones within reach than their computers. The prevalence of mobile devices is certainly a factor, but the usefulness of a simpler interface should not be disregarded; it's an important element in Facebook's big shift to mobile. In fact, other social networks—Pinterest, Yelp, Twitter, LinkedIn, even Facebook's Instagram—aren't shrinking on the web. Facebook just has too much content, and it's becoming overwhelming.

Some pundits argue that Facebook must find a way to make its mobile sites more robust. These are generally the same people who argue that Facebook needs to grow at all costs to succeed. Facebook seems to agree with this view and is unfortunately taking on the challenge with new feature-rich products. I couldn't disagree more with this approach. Facebook will open itself up to competition if it doesn't give users what they want without having to wade through the muck.

Google launched Google+ in 2011 and made a strong attempt to avoid the pitfalls of previous social networks. There are no ads and no spam, and Google+ encourages people to connect only with their closest friends. Here is how Bradley Horowitz, vice president of product for Google+, places it in the context of Facebook: "It's never fun to be late to a market, but it does afford you an opportunity to talk to users. What needs are not being met? What do they like and not like? We believe in the online world you should be able to have a conversation with your cycling buddies that stays with your cycling buddies."

Unlike Google+, Twitter doesn't limit connections, yet it does excel at simplicity. While Twitter is much smaller than Facebook in terms of number of users and time spent on the platform, it is growing quickly. Twitter is particularly well suited for the mobile world, and its usage stats bear this out. Twitter users spent about two hours per month on the Twitter app or mobile website, but only about 20 minutes on twitter.com via their PCs. But both versions continue to grow.

Twitter's very nature minimizes distractions. With only 140 characters to share with the world, you'd better get to the point.

Another way Twitter keeps your feed fluff-free is in its system of "followers" rather than friends. On Facebook, when you accept someone's friend request, they can see your posts and you can see theirs. It's a handshake, a mutual relationship. Not so with Twitter, which means that if April Ridmoore wants to follow you, she's more than welcome, but you're under no obligation to do the same. You don't have to make the awkward choice of whether to deny or perpetually ignore her friend request.

The Twitter information model works more similarly to that of the brain. Each neuron has inbound connections and outbound connections. Sometimes one neuron is connected to another through both an inbound and an outbound link, but not always. Information travels strictly in the most useful direction, and no neuron gets her feelings hurt if another neuron doesn't reciprocate her outbound connection. Noise and distraction are minimized; tasks are performed efficiently; everyone is happy.

I'm not suggesting that Twitter or Google+ will overtake Facebook. On the contrary, I believe that Facebook has a future in social networking, but perhaps not as the huge beast it has become. Facebook is currently synonymous with social networking, and that's its value proposition. In the future, social networking won't be a destination; it will be deeply integrated into everything that we do. There will not be another giant; the future of social networking is smaller, more specific (i.e., less noisy) networks. Facebook knows this. Threadsy, Spool, Tagtile, Gowala, Strobe, Friend.ly, Push Pop, Karma, Lightbox, Glancee . . . most of these companies you probably haven't heard of and perhaps you never will because all have been purchased by Facebook, at a cost of billions of dollars.

One of Facebook's most expensive acquisitions is Instagram, which it bought for a hefty $1 billion in 2012. Interestingly,

Facebook made a concerted effort to keep Instagram independent. Zuckerberg explained when the acquisition was announced: "We need to be mindful about keeping and building on Instagram's strengths and features rather than just trying to integrate everything into Facebook." While posting an Instagram picture to your Facebook page is seamless, you could also use Instagram alone (it's a social network in its own right), or with Twitter, Tumblr, Flickr, or foursquare. Zuckerberg was thinking like a brain scientist in allowing Instagram to continue to organically link to other networks. That is, until December 2012, when he changed his mind and severed the tie between Twitter and Instagram. It is very difficult for any company to avoid central command and control.

The future of Instagram will be interesting to watch because it's a combination of both the social networking revolution and a more recent visual revolution. Sharing pictures has been an important part of our social experience for decades. Children of the 1970s and 1980s grew up in the glow of a camera flash, but counted on their parents to develop the film, throw out the bad pictures, and maybe get double prints of the best shots to send to grandma. Children born in the late 1990s and beyond have an entirely different relationship with photojournalism: they expect that their every moment will be photographed, filtered to look more interesting than it actually was, tagged and posted immediately for the world's viewing pleasure. Instagram adjusts pictures for optimal brightness and contrast and then allows users to apply filters to make the photo more beautiful and also to set the mood—maybe add drama with dark shadows or perhaps a little fading for a vintage feel. Like the internet itself, the visual revolution is already changing not only how we communicate, but also how we see ourselves.

Pinterest is the new social networking kid on the block, and it's also part of this visual revolution. It has yet to be acquired by Facebook, but I'd bet they are talking. Pinterest emphasizes beautiful pictures of decorations, clothing and accessories, recipes, and the like. You can take a look at someone's Pinterest board and tell something about them, no words required. This is interesting from a perspective of universal communication: while we will ultimately be able to communicate with only our thoughts connected to the internet (no common verbal language required), communicating via photographs—worth a thousand words, after all—is a rudimentary first step. Our photographs tell our stories, so the network of all of our photographs linked together carries a social intelligence that is much greater than the sum of its parts.

III

Of course, there are those who think that social sharing is beyond appalling, just as there have always been those who resist any new technology. Since the mid-1990s, there has been plenty of vocal opposition to the integration of the internet into our lives— the naysayers claim that it threatens to create an irreversible dependency, fundamentally redefining who we are. I couldn't agree more. We are dependent: just recall the sheer panic you felt the last time you misplaced your smartphone. There's just no way to stop it, nor should we want to. Kevin Kelly, founder of *Wired* magazine, puts it this way:

> We're so dependent on [the internet] that I have now gotten to the point where I don't even try to remember things—I'll just Google it. It's easier to do that. And we kind of object at first, saying, "Oh, that's awful." But if we think about the dependency

that we have on this other technology, called the alphabet, and writing, we're totally dependent on it, and it has transformed culture. We cannot imagine ourselves without the alphabet and writing. And so in the same way, we're going to not imagine ourselves without this other machine being there.

When technology becomes ubiquitous, it changes us. Will the internet in general and social networking in particular change the game as dramatically as language? My answer is yes, and they are here to stay. It is a brave new world, one that's permanently changing individuals, politicians, corporations, and governments. It's creating a new kind of winner and a new kind of loser.

To be sure, we've had some epic social media failures. A Canadian woman lost her disability benefits when vacation pictures on Facebook contradicted her claims of debilitating depression. Divorce lawyers now frequently monitor Twitter and Facebook posts to find dirt on their clients' exes, to be used in alimony and child custody negotiations. One mom even lost custody of her children because her Facebook profile showed she was spending too much time playing Farmville. And not a day passes without a handful of people's poor social media judgments getting them fired (for posting party pictures on alleged sick days, for example), or simply not hired (most employers shy away from candidates whose profile picture includes a bottle of tequila in each hand, Cinco de Mayo or not).

Even companies with stellar public relations records have made similar social media gaffes. The SEC decided to investigate Netflix for a potential violation of disclosure rules after its CEO bragged on Facebook that Netflix customers were watching a billion hours of video per month. Or consider this tweet from Kenneth Cole during the height of the revolution in

Egypt: "Millions are in uproar in #Cairo. Rumor is they heard our new spring collection is now available online at http://www .bit.ly/KCairo -KC." Unsurprisingly, the insensitive remark was re-tweeted like wildfire, drawing contempt from the company's foes and friends alike.

Blunders like these occur because of a failure to realize the breadth and depth of social media. Your boss, your constituents, your customers, and, yes, even your ex-wife's divorce lawyer are all connected to you. They are removed from you not by six degrees of separation, but by one mouse click. In addition to breadth, companies and institutions must acknowledge the depth of their social media friends, followers, and subscribers. The people who choose to follow you via social media are the ones who really care. They are Malcolm Gladwell's mavens, and the most social ones are also connectors. If you were a rock star, they would be your groupies. Ignore them or underestimate them at your peril.

Clearly, the idea of your groupies turning against you is terrifying. But many are forging a path to successfully navigate this brave new world. Kanye West's clan largely forgave him when he offered a tweeted apology for snatching the microphone from Taylor Swift at the Grammys. Pepsi quickly apologized via Twitter for an insensitive Pepsi Max ad that depicted "one lonely calorie" committing suicide. By using Twitter instead of traditional media, Pepsi and Kanye were able to reach out quickly and directly to those who mattered most.

Because it is informal, personal, and immediate, social media is well suited for apologies and damage control. If you face negative publicity in new media, there is zero chance of turning it around with old media techniques. A formal company statement just can't compete with a 1-star rating on Yelp or the Facebook group "Boycott Your-Company-Name-Here." In 2009, Domino's was blindsided by a YouTube video showing two disgruntled employees contaminating the food they were about to deliver. It was a PR nightmare for the company until they fired back through social media—uploading their own YouTube video explaining what they were doing to fix the situation and creating a special Twitter account specifically to handle customer concerns about the issue. Because of their quick and appropriate responses directly to the people most concerned, Domino's was able to diffuse what could have been a catastrophic event.

Similarly, in 2011, Taco Bell combated a traditional attack—a class action lawsuit charging that the restaurant's meat isn't really beef—with new-media techniques. On Twitter, Taco Bell linked to comedian Stephen Colbert's musings on the controversy; on Facebook, they offered free tacos, encouraging customers to make up their own minds about the meat in question. And while overall sales took a short-term hit, its seven million loyal Facebook "friends" remained as enthusiastic as ever—and the lawsuit was dropped.

The difference between those who fail and those who succeed in the age of social media is simple. Success is no longer about fancy packaging and carefully controlled messages. When everyone can see what you're doing, the most essential values are transparency, honesty, and credibility. Even with advanced privacy tools—like private lists, tweets, and circles—the most foolproof way to stay safe on social media is simply to be who you say you are. Pretending to be something you're not, or attempting to conceal or manipulate the truth, is a surefire way to lose. You win by matching your image with reality, acting with integrity, and apologizing sincerely when you are wrong.

IV

Perhaps the most interesting thing about social media is the lack of a hierarchical structure. Because no one is in charge, users inevitably take control and make the network their own. The term "tweet" was coined not by Twitter but by users, and Twitter's now infamous hashtag (the # sign) was also created organically, by users for users. The lack of an organizational structure certainly allows for many blunders and mistakes, but it also enables tremendous efficiency, growth, and progress.

Like social networks, none of the world's millions of ant colonies has any type of central command. Despite the fact that we call her the queen, the mother ant does nothing more than lay eggs. There is no parent, no president, no central command. As a CEO of a large company, it is hard not to find this intriguing, with some pretty serious suggestions for organizational management. Are we better off just laying eggs (ideas?) and staying out of the way?

True networks don't have leadership, and true networks seem to last longer than companies, governments, and other hierarchies. To study the greatest organizations is to study networked organizations.

SIX

CHIEFS | SEARCH | CONTEXT

In 1999 Marissa Mayer graduated from Stanford with two computer science degrees and a specialization in artificial intelligence. Faced with an overwhelming 14 job offers, it would have been a no-brainer for Mayer to accept the most lucrative position, possibly the one from Oracle or Carnegie Mellon or even McKinsey. Yet the one offer that intrigued her most was from Google, a startup with only 19 employees and even less revenue, but overflowing with passion and excitement. When weighing her options, Mayer says she thought back to other good life decisions she had made and analyzed what they had in common. "In each case, I'd chosen the scenario where I got to work with the smartest people I could find . . . And the other thing was I always did something that I was a little not ready to do. In each of those cases, I felt a little overwhelmed by the option. I'd gotten myself in a little over my head."

So Mayer passed on the prestigious university job and the lucrative consulting gig and started work at Google headquarters in a small office on a quiet street in Palo Alto close to Stanford's campus. She joined as employee number 20 and took on the task of designing a homepage for the budding search engine.

After analyzing the designs of hundreds of search engines and websites, Mayer decided that a change was needed. Back then, most websites were filled with information, links, and clutter. There was little organization, and the structure was complex. Simplicity, she decided, would be Google's differentiator. Mayer was the one who created the now ubiquitous Google homepage: a search box and a button, nothing more. The "I'm feeling lucky" button came later, but little has changed since then in the interface of the search engine. Mayer explained it this way: "Google should be . . . clean, simple, the tool you want to take everywhere."

Mayer and the team at Google famously upended the world of search, the gateway to the World Wide Web. Their innovations started with a new search algorithm, one that replicated the way the brain works. They compared website links to neuronal links and completely reorganized the web as a result. But they went a step further and focused on how the searchers (computers) worked with those who were searching (us mortals). It worked. They toppled the old regimes, led by Yahoo! and a fleet of other sites that no longer exist.

So it came with great irony when Yahoo! asked Marissa Mayer to be their new CEO in 2012. By 2012, most people ruled out Yahoo! entirely. Once a mighty company, Yahoo! was dying, evidenced by declining revenues, de minimis market share, and declining users. Yahoo! had massively overshot the breakpoint of their environment, and everyone—including the company's leadership—had left the search business for dead. The team went so far as to pawn off the entire search product to their once formidable competitor, Microsoft. Yet Mayer accepted the role. She clearly saw things differently.

And maybe we should as well. It is easy to rule out companies simply because they seem behind the curve, but in business it is often as bad to be early as it is to be late. Sometimes a company is actually ahead of the curve and we just can't see it. Sometimes we see decline when what is actually happening is a technology overshooting on its way to equilibrium.

We also often forget that *people* are behind most technological innovations and that a great leader and visionary can change everything. Consider Apple. The company was a shining star that quickly faded. The story unfolded in a remarkably prescient way: the company focused on proprietary technology that turned out to be too simple to compete in the digital age. Their designs were beautiful but not functional, and they were downright hard to work with. So the board of directors fired their enigmatic CEO, Steve Jobs, and replaced him with a string of dogmatic managers. The result was a company in ruins, technology in peril, stock with little value, and a business with no hope for the future.

Then a funny thing happened. Steve Jobs returned to Apple and brought the company back to its original luster. In the process, he turned it into the biggest company in the world. In part, it was because Apple began to innovate again. But most of the success was a result of looking back to the future. Jobs returned Apple to its fundamentals: simple, elegant design, totalitarian control over the hardware and software, and relentless competition. This time around, the world was ready for Jobs's vision, and Apple blossomed.

Individual CEOs are often given far too much credit for their company's success. But occasionally, individuals can make a real difference. In these cases, success comes as a result of a CEO's passionate focus on a singular vision. It is often marked first with failure, a look into an abyss, before emerging ultimately more successful than before. It's a breakpoint in its own right. That was the case with Apple and so too was it the case with Google. The question to ask is whether Mayer was a key component of Google's success and whether she can drive Yahoo! forward by looking back to its future.

|

Yahoo! started life as "Jerry's Guide to the World Wide Web," which was almost as unsophisticated as it sounds. It was the brainchild of David Filo and Jerry Yang, two Stanford PhD students who built the guide to share their favorite websites with their fellow students. Early iterations of the site were merely David and Jerry's lists of favorites, broken down into categories and subcategories. Real people, intelligently choosing the web's best content to present to others.

Despite its humble origins, Yahoo! positively exploded, going from zero to one million hits a day in less than a year. As its user base grew, so did demand for more and more content. What started out as a sparse white page with a single alphabetical list of categories grew into a dynamic, feature-rich one-stop shop. It was made for surfing and exploring. It wasn't a search engine; in fact, it was meant to eliminate the *need* for a search engine. Yahoo! was a web portal, a kind of "welcome to the internet" home page, and in 1994 this was desperately needed. The average user had no idea what was available on this newfangled "internet"—she needed a tour guide, and Yahoo!'s portal filled that role. Search wasn't a key component because no one had any idea what to search for.

Imagine landing for the first time on a brand-new planet, about which you know nothing. You wouldn't step out of your spaceship and start looking for tigers. You don't even know if there are any tigers, or if that is what you should call them if they do exist. You would more likely want a tour guide to escort you to see the most interesting, worthwhile features of the planet. Especially when getting from one place to another would take several minutes of the limited time you had before someone inevitably picked up the telephone and inadvertently knocked you off the planet.

As people became more familiar with the internet, the need for a tour guide decreased. People started using the internet to find specific information, and with that shift, the search box became a vital feature. Search engines popped up like gophers: Lycos, Excite, Altavista, Magellan, Infoseek, DogPile. These search engines had a singular goal—index as many pages as possible. Early search engines organized the content of webpages by keywords, which were used to search on a massive scale. The more pages a search engine had indexed, the better. Google started out using this model as well. While founders Larry Page and Sergey Brin were still at Stanford, Google was already crawling almost fifty pages per second and was able to index sites even faster than that.

In the 1990s, none of the search engines were particularly dominant. In fact, in 1996, when Netscape wanted to make a deal with a single search engine for its web portal, it ended up making a deal with five of them and using them in rotation. But by the year 2000, when Yahoo! sought a similar deal, Google was its clear choice. Remember, Yahoo! was never, and still isn't, a search engine—it was created as a portal to the best of the internet, selected by people, not generated by machines. Yahoo! did initially have a search bar, but it only searched its own directory, not the full contents of the web.

Most people think that search engines are about finding information—even the word "search" begs to be paired with "find." And that's what first-generation search engines did. They found as many pages as possible. However, in a world where several billion pages are added to the web every single day—some good, some great, but most completely worthless—the primary goal of search engines is to filter. Not to find, but to eliminate.

Google, named after the massive number you get when you take 10 to the 100th power, made a fundamental shift in focus from quantity of pages indexed to quality of search results. The need for this became more apparent as the internet grew. Not coincidentally, that's the same thing the brain does when it recalls or searches for information. It assigns appropriate value to what's important and discards everything else.

On the internet, how do you figure out what to filter and what to keep? How can a computer program tell what humans will find most valuable? Google shepherded in a new generation of search with a simple concept to solve these problems: the importance of a website is directly proportional to how many other websites link to it. And it is a matter not only of the *number* of links but also the *quality* of those links; the thinking being that the best websites should have many other reputable websites that link to them. This harks back to "Jerry's Guide to the World Wide Web," where Jerry himself judged the quality of websites and put them on the list if he liked them. Only on Google, Jerry is replaced by the millions of webmasters who create each site and choose their links. The idea is that if a webmaster links to a page, he endorses it.

There are millions of Jerrys, and Google essentially uncovers the recommendations of each one and aggregates the results to rank each website and determine whether a user will see that page first, fifteenth, or four hundredth. The result is that the sites with the best links are presented in the search results first. Of course, once a site gets to the top of Google (the goal of anyone with a website these days), it becomes even more popular and gets more links.

Does that sound familiar? It should, because that is how the brain works: the best neurons, those with the richest connections, have the most links to other neurons around them. With Yahoo!, Jerry was the brain behind the search engine; with Google, the internet itself acts as the brain.

In their own way, Google's algorithms are mimicking the brain's need to clear out the clutter and find the good stuff. Google's method for assessing link relevance works precisely the way a simple neural network does. Links between neurons are weighted based on how relevant (or connected) they are to one another, and that weighting triggers or suppresses activity. Google uses a similar structure to rank or suppress websites through its search results.

It's no surprise that Google's algorithms mimic the brain. Larry Page's PhD advisor was Terry Winograd, well known not only as a professor of computer science at Stanford but also as a leading expert on brain science. Winograd's books—including *Understanding Natural Language, Language as a Cognitive Process,* and *Understanding Computers and Cognition*—explore the possible bridges between human and computer communication. Page, in other words, was well versed in the brain by the time he founded Google. And if Page needed additional explanation of the bonds between cognition, language, and computers, he needed look no further than his own father, Carl Victor Page, who was a professor at Michigan State University and an expert in artificial intelligence.

Even with its first-rate results and solid brain science roots, Google was relatively unknown until Yahoo! pegged it to be the official search engine alongside Jerry's Guide and introduced Google to millions of users in 2000. You have to wonder if Yahoo! knew at the time that it had just given its most formidable competitor a formidable leg up.

||

In the first decade of the twenty-first century, Google started churning out product after product, many of them under the leadership of Marissa Mayer. And while the primary driver of Google's traffic is search, it has become a portal in its own right, with news, videos, free email, maps, and the like. So even the world's most superior search engine company has diversified to provide more of what users need from the internet. As Mayer explained while at Google, "what you want, when you want it. As opposed to everything you could ever want, even when you don't."

At its heart, search has always been a conduit, a translator, between a human with a question and a machine that may or may not have the answer. This is a basic human need; it is what drove us to language formation and more complex forms of communication. Humans evolved complex tools for storing information within our own brains and across those of our peers. Communication enabled us to not only share information, but also retrieve it. Searching was one of the brain's great innovations, allowing us to learn, adapt, and transfer knowledge from one generation to the next. Search was an early brain function to be sure—the newer brain regions responsible for things like consciousness utilize other tools. But search allowed us to expand our cognition beyond that of the animal kingdom. As we created new ways to

expand that reach, we leveraged them with ever-increasing sophistication, whether it was cave painting, language, printing, or
computing.

The exponential growth of the internet brought about a similar challenge to that of the brain: how to categorize and recover
all that information. The search engine has been the answer to
that need for the past two decades, and Google has dominated
that answer. Google simply has the best algorithms that produce a
list of the websites most likely to be able to answer your question.
Its algorithms best match those in our heads, so they provide a
natural solution.

Many companies have challenged Google's dominance, but so
far none has succeeded. The streets of Silicon Valley are littered
with the corpses of the various search engines that have tried to
beat Google at its game of producing great search results. Out of
reverence for the dead (and having run one myself), I won't men-
tion these companies. But even Google is not indestructible.

There are a few hot new search challengers that have some
different ideas about search results. Blekko's claim to fame is that
it doesn't have any advertising, a slap in the face to Google's sponsored results. It also filters out any information provided by non-
authoritative sources, cleverly dubbed "content farms." Wolfram
Alpha considers itself a "computational knowledge engine" that
answers factual questions directly instead of providing a list of
links. DuckDuckGo, in addition to featuring a cute cartoon duck
in its ultraclean interface, uses information from sites like Wikipedia to augment traditional search results. So when I search for
"Santa Monica," it tells me that "Santa Monica is a city in west-
ern Los Angeles County, CA, US," before giving me a list of links.

Google's answer to these competitors is Knowledge Graph,
a side panel without embedded ads that shows up with facts and

content about a topic instead of search results. These are serious threats—and Google treats them as such—despite the silly names. Could Blekko, DuckDuckGo, or even Google 2.0 become the next Google? It's unlikely. Google has largely won the search wars. Its kinks, unfortunately for these search startups, are not in search. Google's problems are more long term, but also more fundamental. And these problems will ultimately lead to the demise of Google search and the rise of a host of new search technologies.

III

The real innovations in search will be more fundamental than filtering out spam or spitting out facts instead of links. The search revolution will consist of battles on three fronts. First, search engines will incorporate context to personalize results. Second, the human–machine interface will be perfected, and the search box will be eliminated. And finally, the demand for search will drastically decline as we turn to specialized apps and ultimately find the answers to our questions without search.

Today, the major problem to be solved for Yahoo!, Google, and all the smaller, hungrier web companies is far beyond page rankings and light years beyond crawling millions of sites. It's about giving users what they want, when they want it, where they want it—and no one knows this better than Marissa Mayer.

Mayer held half a dozen titles at Google, but her last role, the one Yahoo! plucked her from, was VP of Local, Maps, and Location Services. Now, if you haven't used Google Maps in the past few years, the only plausible explanation is that you haven't left your house. This is an application that aspired to replace paper maps and grew into software that actually tells you where to go and where your friends are, in addition to how to get there with the least amount of traffic. No traditional paper map ever told you that Mike's Café at the next exit has a five-star review for its grilled cheese and that if you don't stop for gas now, the next station is 25 miles away. This technology is fundamentally changing our lives and businesses, and the exciting thing is that it's in its infancy. In the next generation of search, context and personalization will reign supreme.

Humans know that the context of the question matters. If you ask a friend where to go to see jaguars, there is very little chance that, knowing you love cars, he'll direct you to the zoo. Unless, of course, you both happen to be on safari in South America, in which case he would be crazy to send you to a car dealership. He also won't send you to a dealership in Seattle, knowing you live in Los Angeles. Your friend intuitively understands the context because he knows *where* you are and *who* you are—your job, your hobbies, your family, your location, your other friends. It's just easier to communicate with, and more fun to be around, people who know us. This is what humans do, and this is why we make and maintain friendships. Our brains are prediction engines, wired to connect disparate facts into coherent thoughts. Context allows us to make that happen.

Facebook is working to personalize a user's search experience in just this way. It should come as no surprise that the effort is being led by a gaggle of Googlers. Roughly 10 percent of Facebook's staff once worked at Google. Why? Because many of the brains at Google have already realized that the world of search has changed. If context matters, then search needs to evolve to incorporate one's place in space and time. These days, there is nowhere better to do that than on Facebook.

Facebook organically creates search-like results by allowing users to ask natural questions of friends and receive conversational results. This happens through their feeds, profiles, status, and timeline. At one point, Facebook tried to link all of this contextual search to an advertising product called Beacon. It was a huge disaster precisely because it worked so well. Imagine the mixed emotions of a woman finding out about an imminent marriage proposal by Beacon suggesting that she consider looking for a wedding dress given that her boyfriend just bought an engagement ring!

If your best friend tells you on Facebook that you absolutely must try Wolfgang Puck's new restaurant, come Saturday night, you probably won't be Yelping Puck's restaurant reviews, let alone searching for a different restaurant. You'll just head out to see what Wolfgang is cooking up. This is the concept behind Chacha and Mahalo, "human-guided" search engines. We should do what we have always done and ask our friends or proxies for friends. Luckily, our friends proficiently tweet, follow, and like, and will soon pin, check-in, and stamp as well. The rise of social sharing and recommending threatens to undermine the very concept of search. If the internet can take in all this social information and combine it with personalized context, perhaps it will have an answer for you even before your friends do.

Remember, Google now has Google+, its own social network, which allows it to use conversations between friends to create context in its search engine. But that is not a solution in itself any more than were previous social networks. Just linking people together doesn't necessarily add context. Facebook pushes recommendations, alerts, and messages through natural conversation, and as of 2013 started developing its own search product, called Facebook Graph Search, to help users find information based on their networks of friends without using a traditional search engine. Google is inevitably tied to its search box for the foreseeable future. While it could conceivably incorporate a friend's feedback into search results, that method leads to an awkward conversation at best.

Many other companies are busy trying to make the machine appear to each user as if it's an old friend. If you are searching for jaguars from the San Diego Zoo with FourSquare, Yelp, or Dartmouth's Hapori, the engines will send you to the Wikipedia page of the big cat or even a description on the zoo's website. Other upstarts, such as Quora, are going back to basics and creating a Q&A expert to hone in on context. Want to know more about a jaguar? Ask the person who built the car (or bred the cat) . . . a Jerry's Guide for every question. Google, on the other hand, solves this problem by presenting a list of clarifications on the results page and asking you to choose "jaguar the cat" or "jaguar the car."

We're moving toward search becoming a kind of personal assistant that knows an awful lot about you. As a side note, some of you may be feeling quite uncomfortable at this point with this new virtual friend. My advice: get used to it. The benefits will be worth it. As Kevin Kelly has said: "Total personalization in this new world will require total transparency. That is going to be the price. If you want to have total personalization, you have to be totally transparent."

IV

It's clear that we are moving into a new era, one in which, if we allow the search engines to get to know us, the answers to our questions will be personalized and contextual. But what about the way we ask the question in the first place? When you strip away the layers of the search problem, you find at its core a communication problem. Humans speaking to machines, and so much ending up lost in translation.

Internet search has always been about text, always about a box in which one could enter words, sentences, and sometimes even questions. But this has never been an ideal interface; it leaves too much between the internet and the individual. Search should be about context, not text.

What if the box could become unbounded? How can we help a person, with all her linguistic nuances, turn questions into computer speak? How can we help a computer, with its cold-hearted calculations, understand the nuances of an emotional machine?

Google finds itself in a tough position. Search is, after all, what Google is all about. Their simple iconic page, with nothing more than a search box, is an integral part of Google's very fabric. As all mammals know, it is hard to chew on your own flesh, even if doing so is needed to survive. But many others are taking advantage of Google's blind spot and going after the meat of the search interface.

And that might be precisely why Mayer left Google. Remember that Yahoo! started without a search box. It was just a list of favorite sites. That worked in the Precambrian days of the web, but by the time the web got big enough, the only technical solution was a search box. So Yahoo! adopted one, quietly giving up all of Jerry's lists. But timing is everything, and there is now an opportunity, once again, to move beyond the status quo. We are already seeing companies big and small enter the fray with a vengeance.

Five years ago, Mayer envisioned this exact scenario and outlined the ideal search engine: "It would be a machine that could answer that question, really. It would be one that could understand speech, questions, phrases, what entities you're talking about, concepts. It would be able to search all of the world's information, different ideas and concepts, and bring them back to you in a presentation that was really informative and coherent." In short, it wouldn't be Google, and it wouldn't look anything like today's search engines.

That was a year before Apple purchased a startup called Siri and two years before it introduced the natural language interface to the world by including it as the central feature in the iPhone 4S. Siri takes Mayer's simple search box to the next logical step by removing the box. Siri is a search engine interface, and she's one of the best we've come up with so far. She allows us to bypass the search box entirely on our phones and instead exchange questions and answers with our devices. We can ask "What's the weather today?" or "How many calories are in a donut?" or "Did the Lakers win?" Depending on the clarity of our speech, we may even receive sensible answers to those questions.

Siri is truly remarkable as one of the first of her species, and she's only going to get better. As anyone who has spent time with her knows, Siri is far from perfect. Despite her intelligence and pleasant demeanor, I have yet to see anyone I know walking around in constant conversation with her (outside of Morgan Freeman, and that is only during a commercial). In fact, sometimes it seems that she's more entertainer than assistant—people love pulling Siri out to share some of her more amusing answers, like "I have no particular insight into the motivations of chickens" when asked "Why did the chicken cross the road?"

Siri isn't the only one who can speak our language. Evi is Siri's half-sister who only speaks to Android users. Evi is similar to Siri but also allows users to agree or disagree with her answers, a crowdsourcing feature that counts on the inputs of thousands of users to help her grow exponentially smarter by the day. In addition to Evi and Siri, there are even a couple of non-mobile–based search engines using natural language, such as Lexxe and Swingly.

The ultimate triumph for these voice-prompted search engines is to understand *who* they are talking to. My five-year-old daughter knows it is me on the phone, even from 3,000 miles away. One day Siri, Evi, and the others will too, and that will ultimately merge this new natural interface with the revolutions happening in contextual search. Nuance, perhaps the largest brain science company in the world, has a new search interface they call Nina that promises to recognize the speaker with pinpoint accuracy. Perhaps one day Nina will be able to give my daughter a run for her money.

The new generation of search will allow us to ask questions in our own natural language, and will provide personalized answers based on context and our unique preferences. We are in the early stages, to be sure, but change is afoot.

The natural consequence of this change is the death of search engines and search altogether. First, the engines. The trend has already turned on the engines. With new devices bursting onto the scene and the applications that come with them, people are using other means to find what they want. For the definition of a word, we use dictionary.com; for an explanation of a topic, we head straight to Wikipedia. If we're curious about what people are saying about Justin Bieber's new album, we head to Twitter. If we're looking for a great gumbo recipe, we ask our Facebook friends. To find a restaurant, we use Yelp, and to browse new houses, we use Trulia or Redfin.

We are finding these things on our smartphones and tablets using apps, bypassing the World Wide Web altogether. The reality is that search was needed only when people didn't know where to start. The web is now better defined, and it's even being truncated into clusters or mini-webs. It's just easier to go directly to appropriate content and bypass the search engine entirely. Not surprisingly, these clusters mimic the modularity of the brain.

Search is an old brain system: it is used more for primitive functions than for cognitive ones. In the brain, we find information through a process of spreading activation, which is a lot like osmosis. We think of something and then other related things come to mind. "Where are my keys?" leads to thoughts of my day, my path, a mental map of my house—a detour through the breakfast I forgot to clean up—then back to the couch in the living room, and voilà, my keys appear in between the cushions. One neuron fires, and that sets off a chain reaction of other nearby neurons. There is no search box, no list of results to choose from.

And then there's this idea: perhaps the internet will feed you an answer before you ask the question. Imagine that the internet can read your thoughts. Your personal computer, now a personal assistant, knows you skipped breakfast, just as your brain knows you skipped breakfast. She also knows you have been in back-to-back meetings but that your schedule just cleared. So she offers a suggestion: "It's 11:00 A.M. and you should really eat before your next meeting. D'Amore's Pizza Express can deliver to you within 25 minutes. Shall I order your favorite, a large thin crust pizza, light on the cheese with extra red pepper flakes on the side?"

This is exciting and life-changing stuff. Next time you enter a keyword into a search bar, think about a world with no more search. Consider how, if the internet knew you a little better, it/he/she could have already provided you the answer before you knew you had the question.

The world of search is rapidly evolving, and the first step is to imagine and then understand what that might mean. Creating businesses, experiences, and new worlds around these changes is where the real fun begins. If we can imagine a world where we are having conversations with our machines, we can understand how to adapt to these natural conversations. With it will emerge new worlds of interaction between mind and machine. If we can imagine a world where the machine can anticipate our needs, we begin to understand how predictions are transformed into actions, with endless possibilities and alternatives. This world is barreling toward us, faster than any of us could have imagined.

SEVEN

CROWDS | POETS | SHAKESPEARE

That a bastard strumpet
Should get ahead in the court
That in love or in wine
Louis should seek easy glory,
Ah! There he is, ah! Here he is,
He who doesn't have a care.

Thus begins one of six illicit poems circulating Paris in 1749. Sometimes recited, sometimes sung to the tunes of popular songs, the poems criticized and mocked King Louis XV and his new mistress. Not known for his sense of humor, the king demanded that the author of the poetry be tracked down and brought to justice for his blasphemy.

The finest detectives in France were assigned to the case, and soon police arrested medical student François Bonis, who had recited one of the poems in his parlor only a week before. However, after hours of questioning, it became clear that Mr. Bonis was not the author. He had copied one of the poems from a visiting priest, Jean Édouard. The police promptly arrested Mr. Édouard and brought him in for questioning. But he claimed that he had heard one of the poems recited by another priest, Inguimbert de Montange. De Montange too turned out not to be the author. The detectives redoubled their efforts. Surely if they followed the trail long enough, they would reach the true insurrectionist.

In the end, fourteen citizens were arrested, imprisoned in the Bastille for months, and ultimately exiled to the French countryside, far away from King Louis. This lot included priests, law clerks, students, and professors—all loyal subjects of the king who fiercely maintained their innocence. And by all accounts, the fourteen were guilty of nothing more than sharing a poem or singing a song in the wrong place at the wrong time.

The fourteen weren't the only ones spreading poetic gossip; the streets of eighteenth-century Paris buzzed with chatter about public affairs. In a society that was only semiliterate, news traveled most effectively by word of mouth. Without the written word, songs containing stories of the day were common because putting news to the tune of a popular song made it easier to remember and share.

The police never found the author of the poems because there was no author. Or to look at it another way, everyone was an author. Someone would start a poem about the day's events, then share it with someone who would recite it but also add their bit, and in turn that person would share it with someone else who would do the same. In a process not unlike that of evolution itself, the most memorable and intriguing pieces of the poem would survive, and the others would be forgotten. This would continue until a memorable song would come of the discord. The citizens of France, as only the French could do, had created the first news network, full of pomp and poetics.

The poems were written by and for the crowd. What started as a couple of cheeky lines quickly became full-scale literary works. The poems spread and grew at a rate that risked a riot or worse. The police had a true dilemma on their hands: they couldn't simply arrest the author because there was no author. But stopping the network that was spreading the poems wasn't an option either—it's almost impossible to slow down a growing network. In either case, obtaining true justice for Louis XV would have meant the arrest and punishment of thousands, which surely would not have been a great public relations move for the unpopular king. The baffled police detectives settled for the next best thing: making examples out of the loudest fourteen in hopes of dissuading others from participating in the crowdsourced network.

|

Crowdsourcing isn't new. From poems to pyramids, collaborative works by groups of people are as old as work itself. But with each new technological innovation, we've brought the crowds closer together. With the proliferation of email, blogs, instant messages, tweets, tags, and pokes, we're now able to communicate with large numbers of people quickly and seamlessly.

The oldest examples of crowdsourcing come from biology. Ants, of course, have a type of swarm intelligence, as do bees, wasps, and other networked insects. If there is a consciousness, a "light in the attic," it is the colony as a whole. The crowd of insects creates swarm intelligence, just as the crowd of individuals created the poetry of 1749 Paris. But just like the Parisian police, we don't really know how they are doing it.

One example of crowdsourcing that we know significantly more about is the human brain. But even there, science has taught us little about exactly how our crowd of neurons creates intelligence, consciousness, and creativity. There are many theories about consciousness but no real answers; the same is true of the other faculties that make humans unique. We believe that the brain is a prediction engine, a pattern recognition machine. We have experiences, we use those experiences to make predictions, and then we guess our way through the world. With each passing guess, we grow wiser. We are prone to fail, fumble, and guess, and that is what makes us intelligent. Brains are unique in their ability to learn through failure. We are more sophisticated versions of the chimps you see on the National Geographic Channel awkwardly groping at tools.

Bumbling baboons is truly what the greatest minds think about our greatest minds. Not surprisingly, even that description is just a guess. The field of neuroscience is too new, too nascent, to give us real insight. What we do know is that our network of neurons acts as a crowd. Each neuron performs a minor task that collectively forms a pattern. We see a snake and certain neurons fire. The snake bites us and other neurons fire. The next time we see a snake, both sets of neurons fire—we see the pattern—and then something unexpected happens: an entirely new group of neurons fire, the ones that make us jump. The scale at which this happens is truly epic: this minor interchange requires tens of millions of neurons firing in a linked chain of events. Just as the crowd of subjects passed King Louis's poem from poet to poet, each neuron fires in response to other neurons.

Our intelligence comes from all of those little charges in our head going on and off in a constant stream, eventually leading to actions that define us. We are greater than the sum of our parts: a result of swarm intelligence, a collective consciousness. It's like a series of dominoes that fall only to reveal a pattern. It's an unbelievable idea when you think about it.

II

Crowdsourcing operates under the assumption that the sum is greater than the parts. Oftentimes this is true, especially in matters where public opinion is important. Advertisers have been using focus groups and surveys for decades—in such instances, the wisdom of the crowd is considered sacred. Complex technical problems have also found solutions through the crowd; open source software like Linux and Apache, for example, is dependent upon crowdsourcing. Crowdsourcing was even used by the British government in 1714 when it held a contest offering £20,000 to whoever could come up with a vacuum-sealed pocket watch (the result was the first marine chronometer).

In the past ten years, crowdsourcing has expanded into new territories. We're relying on crowds to an extent that could not have been predicted even a few decades ago. King Louis XV was incredulous that a crowd could write a poem; imagine his reaction if you told him that we created a 22-million entry encyclopedia with no author.

That encyclopedia, Wikipedia, is the first massive-scale online crowdsourcing platform. More than just a digital reference book, it's a living entity, simultaneously creating and surviving in its own ecosystem of drafts, edits, and interpretive processes. In 2012, Wikipedia contained over 22 million articles in 285 languages (only 4 million of the articles are in English). The entire process is free: its army of 77,000 contributors and editors are all volunteers; its legion of almost half a billion monthly users pays nothing to use the site. It is bigger than the print versions of Britannica, Cambridge, and Americana combined and has put all three out of business permanently. It is truly a global information amalgamation, and it has no author.

Wikipedia had a meteoric growth stage. It grew rapidly from its birth in 2001 to age five, with the number of articles rising exponentially as the total number of words approached two billion (in contrast, the entire *Encyclopedia Britannica* was only about 50 million words). But lately, life hasn't been easy for this global knowledge network. It is currently growing at less than half the rate of 2006 in terms of new content. Founder Jimmy Wales told the press in 2011 that the site was losing contributors and having trouble attracting new ones.

Back in 2007, the network hit a breakpoint and growth began to slow. Contributors and edits peaked, as did the number of new articles, at a staggering 60,000 per month. The site had over 10,000 new editors joining every month, but by 2008, Wikipedia was losing 1,500 per month, and that number jumped to negative 15,000 by 2009. The network itself was starting to crack.

Of course, part of the reason for the decline is surely that there is only so much content to record, and the low-hanging fruit has already been picked. In the early days, a Beatles enthusiast would have been thrilled to contribute information to build the pages of Paul, George, John, and Ringo, and perhaps even a page for Yoko Ono. Now, Wikipedia is so comprehensive that there simply isn't much historical information left to provide.

In many ways, this is analogous to the amount of carrying capacity available. Wikipedia peaked and, in doing so, exceeded its carrying capacity. In 2007, the number of editors and new pages hit their breakpoint and began a quick, sharp decline. Since then, the Wikipedia growth curve looks exactly like our breakpoint model.

Despite the concern of Wikipedia's founder, the decline led to stabilization, just as we have seen with all other networks that naturally hit a breakpoint. In spite of the content decline, usage

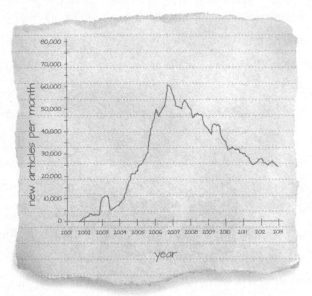

Image 7.1: The Breakpoint of Wikipedia

increased, and Wikipedia remains the sixth most visited website in the world. This is despite the onslaught of Google, Facebook, Twitter, and the many other up-and-comers. Smaller, slower growth in content may just be Wikipedia's secret weapon.

Growth is particularly important to a crowdsourced network like Wikipedia. Crowds need critical mass. Ten or even 1,000 articles won't drive anyone to a site (imagine a dictionary with only 1,000 entries); rapid growth is necessary to become a universal resource. However, there's a point where maintaining hypergrowth in terms of quantity decreases the usefulness of the site. Wikipedia has already reached this point, and now it must focus on quality, not quantity.

Yet in 2011, the Wikimedia Foundation released a five-year strategic plan that made clear that their main focus was growth.

By 2015 they hope to more than double Wikipedia's size to 50 million total articles and 200,000 active contributors per month. They even started hiring recruiters to bring people to the free, nonprofit crowdsourced site. What could be more contrary to the concept of a natural crowd than recruiting? To be sure, there is plenty of room for Wikipedia to grow in different languages—there are a mere 77,000 articles in Thai and 11,000 in Yiddish. But to force growth in terms of Wikipedia's articles and contributors goes against everything we know about the breakpoint of networks.

Consider the value of a print encyclopedia. Sadly for many, *Encyclopaedia Britannica* stopped the presses after printing its final edition in 2010, after 244 years of annual publishing. When asked about the threat of Wikipedia, Britannica's president Jorge Cauz explained that his encyclopedias were very different from Wikipedia, the former set apart by "its prestigious sources, its carefully edited entries and the trust that was tied to the brand." There is plenty of truth to that statement, but Cauz underestimated the intelligence of the crowd. Wikipedia inches closer toward the Britannica model each time the crowd corrects an error or deletes a page. And of course, Wikipedia has huge advantages in that it doesn't weigh 129 pounds or cost almost $1,400.

Since 2006, commentators have been saying that Wikipedia is dying. Mathias Schindler, a board member of Wikipedia in Germany, recently echoed this sentiment: "The number one headline I have been seeing for five years is that Wikipedia is dying." Really, it is improving in quality and reaching equilibrium, and it must be allowed to do so. Crowdsourcing is great for rapid growth, and perhaps great for spreading anti-government poetry, but not always so fantastic for improving quality.

This was Cauz's main insight, but what he may not have fully understood is that size matters first for a crowdsourced network. Wikipedia's hypergrowth allowed it to temporarily leapfrog the old model of quality by offering something where there was nothing. Compared to Wikipedia, the printed *Encyclopaedia Britannica* was simply missing too much information. Interestingly, Jorge Cauz has since reinvented Encyclopaedia Britannica for the digital age by navigating these waters. The company's online encyclopedia is updated continuously and accepts user input that is vetted by expert editors. This has led to record profitability.

Wikipedia could learn from Encyclopaedia Britannica's new model. To grow in quality, the crowd must subside. As Carnegie Mellon professor Aniket Kittur put it, "People generally have this idea that the wisdom of crowds is a pixie dust that you sprinkle on a system and magical things happen. Yet the more people you throw at a problem, the more difficulty you are going to have with coordinating those people. It's too many cooks in the kitchen." Once you have sufficient growth, pulling back paradoxically drives momentum forward.

III

Wikipedia is habitually considered the first crowdsourced reference tool, but another, more prominent example predates it. In the late 1970s, Professor James Murray was tasked by the Oxford University Press with a unique opportunity: to create a dictionary that "by the completeness of its vocabulary, and by the application of the historical method to the life and use of words, might be worthy of the English language and of English scholarship." The idea was interesting in that most dictionaries at the time largely ignored colloquial and scientific words, and nearly all of them left out the history of words.

Oxford's proposal presented a number of challenges for Murray. First, there were already a number of English dictionaries available, so a new one would need to be unique. Second, dictionaries were expensive and time consuming to produce. Finally, a dictionary carrying the Oxford name would need to be superior to all others.

Instead of authoring a new dictionary, a novel strategy was employed: a crowd of colleagues was enlisted to create the entries. Murray's own role was not to create the dictionary; instead, he simply became editor at large. By doing it this way, Murray eliminated the costs of having experts and leveraged the diversity of the masses. Over the first few years, Murray received hundreds of thousands of submissions—slips of papers containing a word and a definition—from tens of thousands of volunteer contributors.

Five years later, the first installment of the *Oxford English Dictionary* was published. Through the turn of the century, work continued on the dictionary until a complete edition was published. It has since become the preeminent English language dictionary and continues to be the gold standard today.

The success of this crowdsourced work is amazing considering that it came before Wikipedia and even the World Wide Web. But that statement diminishes the truly incredible historical context of the story: the *Oxford English Dictionary* wasn't conceived in the twentieth century, it was started 100 years earlier, in 1884! Crowdsourcing is, in fact, very old.

There is something more important than age that sets Murray's dictionary apart from Wikipedia. Whereas Wikipedia's entries are entirely written and edited by the crowd, Murray remained the lead editor overseeing the *Oxford English Dictionary*.

In many ways, this limited Murray's creation, but it also gave it a richness of quality that Wikipedia currently lacks.

Perhaps knowledge networks that involve expert contributions or oversight fare better than ones that rely solely on the wisdom of the crowd. The internet has enabled the proliferation of fan fiction, which consists of stories produced by fans of an existing book, movie, or television show. While written predominantly by a single author, the stories are often posted one chapter or segment at a time, allowing other fans to comment or make suggestions for what follows. Think of it as group editing versus group creation. The popular *Fifty Shades of Grey* trilogy started as *Twilight* fan fiction, and presumably received so much praise that the author was compelled to rewrite the story and incorporate the crowd's feedback into what became bestselling novels in their own right.

Some crowdsourcing networks are taking a high-quality approach even in their growth phases. Academic Room, developed by Harvard University, allows professors to upload files of lectures to be vetted by their peers. A professor uploads a lecture, thousands of people comment, and the lecture is retooled and revamped over time. This process is not unlike academia itself, in terms of how the peer review process works, although the use of the web creates possibilities that few scholars could have previously imagined.

Quora is a question-and-answer website founded by two former Facebook employees. People ask questions, other people answer questions, and users vote the answers up or down. This is a similar model to Yahoo! Answers and Answers.com, but Quora has made a concerted effort toward high quality. The company, which has been around since June 2010, intentionally started very small and then gradually allowed more people to answer questions.

They invited experts to opine, and that method has driven quality over quantity. Ask a question about acting and Ashton Kutcher may answer; ask about business and Mark Zuckerberg may jump in; ask about economics and you may hear from former Harvard president and Secretary of the Treasury Larry Summers. All of these people have posted answers on Quora. The site is in hypergrowth phase in terms of users but not content—they have far fewer answers than most sites, but the quality is so good that Quora is where many people head for the most difficult questions. They are leapfrogging the breakpoint, willing to forgo the size and scale of Wikipedia in order to reach equilibrium faster. No surprise, the team reportedly passed up a $1 billion purchase offer.

There is no question that experts provide knowledge that no crowd can deliver, but the crowd's wisdom should not be underestimated. In *The Wisdom of Crowds,* author James Surowiecki outlined countless situations in which crowds were far better than experts: choosing stocks, deciding the weight of objects, sports betting, even choosing who will be elected president. What sets individual expertise apart from group intelligence is a different type of wisdom. The key driver of expertise is deep experience and knowledge; for crowds, it is diversity. Understanding this is the trick to successfully navigating a breakpoint in a crowdsourced business.

In many ways, it is easier to manage a crowdsourced business through a breakpoint than it is with other networks. After regular networks surpass carrying capacity, it's not always easy to reduce the user base to a manageable number. But with crowds, you have the option to introduce an expert. Quora has utilized this hybrid model brilliantly. They allow crowds to answer a question, but an expert's answer carries added weight and can dictate the direction of the conversation. As Quora grows over time, experts will likely take a more active role in weeding out unnecessary noise.

As Wikipedia's growth began to accelerate, it too leveraged this concept by giving additional powers to more experienced editors. These editors can restrict edits on pages, remove content unilaterally, and even ban other editors from the site. There are inevitably complaints about this practice, but the net effect has been to improve quality and slow unfettered growth post breakpoint.

IV

Crowdsourcing comes in all shapes and sizes online. Just look at the ones that match people needing work done with people seeking employment. Sometimes referred to as "cloud labor," these companies include Elance, oDesk, Guru, CloudCrowd, and Amazon's Mechanical Turk. Even in the deepest recession, it is easy to find jobs on these sites, and many of them can be performed from your own home. While considered crowdsourced, these companies are really just online matchmakers. They are powerful online alternatives to traditional outsourcing, with low transaction fees and the ability to hire workers for even the smallest of jobs. Cloud labor sites allow people to find work and employers to find cost-effective labor.

Since 2007, oDesk has grown by more than 100 percent per year, reaching into over 40 countries. In 2012, there were more than 10,000 new job opportunities each month, totaling $1 billion worth of work. But this isn't like Monster or CareerBuilder; on oDesk, the jobs are single tasks. You might make a call, stuff a few envelopes for the holiday, or assist with a dinner reservation. For that work, you might receive $.25 or $100 and perhaps the opportunity to work again. Whether you are looking for a job in customer service, copywriting, programming, or horse grooming, oDesk has it online.

This fills a critical void in our global economy. Businesses and individuals often need help with tasks that are not large enough for full- or even part-time help. The myriad crowd labor companies address that need. The crowd helps make the labor markets more efficient.

Crowd labor can also be effectively utilized with contests, as has been done since the eighteenth-century British watch competition. Clearly, contests are not new, nor are they purely an internet phenomenon. However, the internet is making it easier for all individuals, companies, and governments to participate.

Netflix offered a million-dollar prize to anyone who could help improve their recommendation engine. It worked: hundreds of programmers, none of whom was actually employed by Netflix, competed to build the best software that could determine what movie you might want to watch with your boyfriend on a rainy Tuesday in July. Similarly, in 2013 GE will award $500,000 in prize money for the team that can create the most effective algorithm for easing plane congestion at major airports. Even small companies are taking advantage of this concept as part of their underlying business model. 99designs, for example, allows clients to submit a brief for a graphic design project, determine prize money for the winner, and then wait for submissions. The average project gets over 100 submissions, and the client pays only for the design he chooses.

The wisdom of the crowd has long been a precious commodity for big business marketers. But the internet has enabled almost every small business to get opinions from the people who matter most. "Social care," as it's been dubbed, refers to providing customer service through Twitter, Facebook, a blog, or a company's website. Sparked.com goes one step further, helping companies create advisory boards of their best customers. Sparked calls itself the heart of the social business revolution, and while that title may be superfluous, social business is certainly a revolution and an indispensable tool for any customer-facing business.

V

In 2012, the world was shocked by a video of Karen Klein, a 68-year-old bus monitor, being bullied to tears by four middle school boys. One man was so moved by the video that he set up an account on crowdfunding site Indiegogo, asking for a total of $5,000 to send Ms. Klein on vacation. Instead, over $700,000 was donated, allowing her to not only go on vacation, but also to retire and set up a foundation to combat bullying.

We've always known that people can be counted on to help others in need—just consider the $64 million donated for victims of Japan's earthquakes, the $145 million given for Hurricane Sandy victims, the $4 billion contributed in the aftermath of Hurricane Katrina. Donation-based crowdfunding via the web adds a few extra dimensions to charitable giving. People want to help and also want to feel part of a community, a network of like-minded souls, if you will. Calling the Red Cross and offering one's credit card number fulfills the first need but not the second.

Joining a crowdfunding community, such as Kiva, Indiegogo, StartSomeGood or Kickstarter, fulfills the desire to give as well as the desire to get involved. President Obama used this to his advantage and leveraged social media and his own crowdfunding website to empower his supporters to donate and participate, and pundits including *New York Times* journalist David Carr even credit that as one of the defining movements that sent Obama to the White House.

It's no surprise that crowdfunding is in hypergrowth despite being a young technology. The 130 existing crowdfunding platforms in the United States raised nearly $3 billion in 2012, almost double the amount they raised the year before. All crowdfunding falls into one of four categories: donation-based, reward-based, lending-based, and equity-based. Donation-based platforms, such as the one used by President Obama, allow people to donate directly to a person or group in need, connect with others who also support the cause, and in many cases receive updates detailing exactly how their money is helping. Reward-based platforms are a slightly different format, often used by independent artists and writers as well as start-up technology companies. They ask contributors to donate money in exchange for some type of good or service. For example, in 2012, musician Amanda Palmer used Kickstarter to raise $1 million to fund her new record. For their contributions, her supporters received a copy of the CD, signed posters, even an in-person meeting. This model is like a presale without the store. An up-front payout enables recording artists and authors to bypass the record label or the publishing house.

Lending-based platforms such as Kiva focus on microloans to small businesses in developing countries; others such as Lending Club enable small-scale investors to lend money to people seeking loans to buy cars, make home improvements, or even plan weddings. Lenders make small loans and group together for bigger amounts. Need $10,000? It may come from 300 people and be facilitated by Lending Club. Lenders receive a healthy return per year and the feeling that they're doing something good; borrowers get to avoid traditional banks and handle the entire transaction in a hassle-free online process. These types of loans are now commonly called microfinancing.

The most controversial type of crowdfunding is equity based, which became legal in the United States when President Obama signed the 2012 JOBS Act. I suspect we'll see hypergrowth in equity-based funding in the next few years, but this type of crowd-sourcing is not without its risks. Hyped as a way to make money fast, equity-based crowdfunding enables just about anyone to invest money in exchange for equity. The advantages of this approach are that it truly democratizes investing in private companies and also makes it easier for new businesses to raise money. The risk is that novice investors could easily become disillusioned when their first few investments tank and they're faced with the reality that becoming Warren Buffet isn't easy. In fact, we've already seen this happening on a smaller scale with Kickstarter projects, where people donate money to companies with the expectation that they will receive a product. CNN found that 84 percent of the site's top projects shipped late, if at all. Kickstarter is trying to combat the impression that the goal of the investment is simply to receive a product. In a 2012 blog post entitled "Kickstarter Is Not a Store," the company's management explained that "it's hard to know how many people feel like they're shopping at a store when they're backing projects on Kickstarter, but we want to make sure that it's no one." So much for the customer always being right. No matter how emphatically stated, Kickstarter's message is a difficult sell. There is little doubt that the nearly 70,000 people who collectively handed over $10.2 million in 2012 for a Pebble Watch, for example, expect to actually receive a watch.

One has to wonder if this type of crowdsourcing is a fun trend, is something for the in-crowd to brag about at dinner parties, or has legs to survive long term. Crowdfunding companies are growing exponentially quarter after quarter, and by all measures, the industry is still in its infancy. At some point, it too will hit a breakpoint.

VI

What a piece of work is a man, how noble in reason, how infinite in faculties, in form and moving how express and admirable, in action how like an angel, in apprehension how like a god: the beauty of the world, the paragon of animals—and yet, to me, what is this quintessence of dust?

We would never expect the words of *Hamlet* to come from a crowd. But scientists have been arguing since the early nineteenth century whether this might be possible. Put enough monkeys in a room with enough typewriters, the argument goes, and eventually they will produce all the works of Shakespeare.

In April 2012, *Time* magazine shared the story of The Collabowriters, a website that was facilitating the writing of the first crowdsourced novel. Anyone can submit his or her idea for the next sentence, and the crowd votes the entries up or down. Once an entry receives enough votes, it becomes part of the novel and the crowd moves to the next sentence. Certainly an interesting concept, but as of early 2013, the novel had only been completed up to page five. In comparison, novelist Stephen King writes five to ten pages per day. *Time* described the novel as "jumpy . . . in a kids-telling-stories-around-a-campfire sort of way." Perhaps crowds have intelligence, but it would seem that literary brilliance is still the domain of individual authors. For now at least, one Shakespeare, even one King, is much better than a thousand crowded poets.

EIGHT

SQUIRTS | PROFIT | TRAFFIC

The first and most important life task of a sea squirt is to find a place to live. These small marine creatures, closely related to hagfish and lampreys, swim around the ocean and weigh the pros and cons of various pieces of real estate. Bits of the seafloor, underwater rocks, and sometimes even the hulls of boats are considered.

When a sea squirt finds the perfect spot, he attaches himself, and it becomes his permanent home. For the rest of his life, the sea squirt will live in this one spot and perform one function: filter in water, remove the plankton to use as food, and filter out what's left. It's automatic, like breathing, and requires little brainpower. Having found a good rock, the sea squirt finds he is no longer in need of the brain that helped him find a home, so he eats it! In doing so, he reduces his energy demands. He'll require far fewer calories in the future than he would have otherwise. Pretty smart.

Consuming his brain works pretty well for the little squirt and his friends: sea squirts have been around since the beginning of the Cambrian period, over 500 million years ago. Every animal's main goal is long-term survival, and like sea squirts, many creatures have evolved unique tricks for that purpose. Wood frogs freeze almost half their bodies and temporarily pause the beating of their hearts when it's too cold to function. Certain carpenter ants, when faced with a serious foe, will squeeze his or her own body until it explodes, unleashing a toxin on the enemy. The ant dies, but in murdering an enemy, it selflessly saves the rest of the colony from that particular threat. The goal of any species, whether frogs, ant colonies, or sea squirts, is to survive as long as possible at any cost.

|

All of an animal's traits, tools, tricks, and so-called advantages are there only to help the species achieve nature's ultimate goal: survival. For our part, humans are almost the opposite of sea squirts: our most unique survival tool is our superior intelligence. We can't run fast like cheetahs; we don't have forceful jaws like crocodiles; our skin isn't camouflaged like that of stonefish or flounder. The one competitive advantage we have is our big brains. Like all animals, the goal of humans is also to survive, and our brains help us do this.

There is an important life lesson within biology: know the end game before you set out on your journey. Enamored with our own intelligence, it is easy for us to forget that if it is not useful for survival, nature will phase it out. The process of evolution eliminates traits when they are costly but not useful: humans lost significant body mass to allow more energy to flow to our brains; turtles lost large spikes on their necks to allow them to retreat into their shells; sharks lost the heavy bone structure of fish in favor of more efficient cartilage.

We have focused up to this point on the phases of networks: how they grow, what happens when they reach breakpoint, and how to keep them from collapsing and enable equilibrium. But more fundamentally, networks seek survival. In fact, this is the only goal of a biological network. When we consider networks run by businesses, however, survival is only one side of the equation. The other is making money. The problem is that these two goals are often at odds.

Businesses are sometimes focused on making money at the wrong time, and it costs them in terms of network growth. Other times, businesses are far too consumed with network growth, and they overshoot to the point of collapse. While growth is critical to a network, it is not an end goal. And while money is critical to any business, it too must sometimes retreat behind the greater goal of survival.

In the first network phase, growth should be pursued at the expense of everything else. The reason is simple: if you don't capture all of the carrying capacity in an environment, someone else will. However, as we've seen, when the network hits a breakpoint, growth should be allowed to slow, and occasionally a forced slowing may be needed. After breakpoint, continued growth will be counterproductive and will cause a network to exceed its carrying capacity.

As a network reaches equilibrium during the final phase, the real rewards start to come in. Equilibrium makes longevity easier— the network is stable, fully scaled, and healthy. But more than that, stable networks can be exploited, and there are many ways to profit from them. It is worth spending some time on each of these stages to explore how they can be managed successfully by businesses.

II

There isn't much that hasn't been said about the growth phase of technological networks. It has been one of the most popular themes for technology books, has become legendary in stories and movies about internet mavens, and has led to untold riches for countless twenty-somethings. Of course, the one missing component in most of these anecdotes is that growth always comes to an end eventually.

Despite the spectacular success of some, the truth remains that most networks (and businesses) die during their growth phase. They simply don't grow enough: they don't catch on, they don't reach hypergrowth, or they don't grow to fill all available carrying capacity. They don't claim their big rock, and this enables competitors to swoop in.

The most successful networks are allowed to grow unencumbered during their growth phase. As we know, networks must have large numbers. Consider that the first telephone was utterly useless. The second phone was slightly more useful, but only to communicate with the first. It took thousands of telephones before purchasing one made sense, and millions more before the telephone became truly indispensable. So it is with any new network. It must grow, and grow, and grow.

Those who run networks should remove all barriers during the growth phase. The object of a business during this time is to gain as many users, as much content, as much lichen, as much of anything that the network needs to thrive and grow. Anything that may create a barrier to growth should be removed. Salaries and costs should be kept low; speeds should be optimized; simplicity is preferable to depth.

By far the largest barrier to growth is money. In keeping with the basic economic theory of demand, charging money shrinks growth. Demand for a product or service goes down as the price goes up. To encourage high demand, prices must be kept low. For the majority of internet networks, it's not enough for the price to be low: it must be free.

Free is the golden rule for pricing during growth. Studies by economists such as Duke University's Dan Ariely have shown that people do not behave rationally when things are offered for free. Among other things, Ariely demonstrated that the difference between free and a penny is often psychologically greater than the difference between $.99 and $1.00, and that affects purchasing behavior. You would think the average smartphone or tablet user wouldn't hesitate to spend money on an app. But a 2012 Cambridge University study found that free apps are 100 times more likely than paid apps to be downloaded more than 10,000 times, despite the fact that the average price of a paid app is only $.99. In fact, only 20 percent of paid apps are downloaded more than 100 times. When something is free, consumers are willing to try it more often and be far less critical.

All of this begs the question of how a company gives away the store and still survives. Two factors are at work here. First, when a person joins an online network, the added cost is often insignificant. My joining Instagram, for example, doesn't cost Instagram anything. Software is especially well suited to being free; once the software is developed, the cost of providing it to additional people is nil. This gives software companies an opportunity that other companies don't have: Ferrari wouldn't survive very long if it started giving away sports cars.

The second factor is venture capital funding. Venture capitalists, no strangers to risk, are often willing to subsidize a company in the short run in hopes of big returns later. In Silicon Valley, many start-up networks attract venture capitalist funding in their hypergrowth phases whether or not the company is generating revenue. Venture capital lives and thrives in the growth phase. Venture money often acts as a subsidy so that consumers don't have to pay for products early in their life cycle. Think of the last time you paid for Twitter, Facebook, LinkedIn, Google, Yahoo!, or any other online service. In the early days, none of these companies made any money; their sole purpose was to satisfy customers and increase their user bases. Money came instead from venture capitalists hoping to reap the long-term rewards of a thriving network.

The odds of succeeding in venture capital are extremely low. That shouldn't surprise anyone given that the odds of success for anything in the growth phase are low—most species and businesses never make it through this period. The best venture firms have a success rate of only 30 percent; the average is below 10 percent. But in many cases, that is enough. A single start-up that makes it through the breakpoint can fuel the success of an entire venture fund. Over 90 percent of companies die during this phase, but venture capitalists thrive on the remaining crop.

Regardless of how much money you can raise, giving your product away for free is counterintuitive to business. It's no wonder that the best network builders of the internet age have been kids: Mark Zuckerberg started Facebook while in college, as did Sergey Brin and Larry Page with Google, and David Filo and Jerry Yang with Yahoo!. With few obligations, kids are willing to work long hours and risk what little they have for long-term potential. Without experience, the absence of revenue doesn't seem so bad. With the reality of an enormous failure rate, younger people also have the benefit of time: they can pick themselves up and try again until they make it.

Sometimes you have no choice but to charge, as is generally the case with physical goods. But even in those cases, it pays to subsidize and sometimes even to lose money. This was true of the early days of almost all the e-commerce giants, from Amazon to Zappos to Netflix. They raised venture capital and used that money to pay their bills while the companies were still unprofitable. E-commerce is still subsidized today, with free shipping and no sales tax in many cases.

Companies that charge too quickly inevitably fail in the long run. AOL charged for internet access right at the start, which allowed room for the free ISPs that nibbled away at AOL's dominance. Consider Peapod, which launched the first grocery delivery network in 1989. In the early days, they charged a hefty sum. While they grew quickly, they failed to make it through the breakpoint. By the mid-1990s, during the heyday of the internet boom, new competitors such as Kosmo and Webvan were taking advantage of this, raising hundreds of millions in venture funding. These competitors quickly overtook Peapod with a more attractive offer: free delivery.

Webvan became a bona fide Wall Street darling; it went public with a mere $15 million in revenues but received an astronomical $8 billion valuation only months later. On the other hand, Peapod had lost its allure. *Morningstar* reported that "investors hate Peapod stock as much as children loathe broccoli." Peapod responded by matching the free delivery offer, but it was too late. Its competitors had secured a commanding position.

Luckily for Peapod, the dot-com crash of 2000 took funding away from its competitors. That allowed Peapod to inch its way back in and learn from its mistakes. Once it dominated the network, Peapod was able to charge again, and the company announced that intention in 2001, weeks after their competitors went bankrupt. Peapod is now the lone standing grocery delivery service at scale. But even today, Peapod's model includes a free component—they will do your shopping and bag up your selected groceries free if you come to the store to pick up the order. Only if you want your order delivered do they charge a fee.

This "freemium" model has become very popular. The idea is that a company creates two classes of product, a free version and a premium version. It can be a great strategy during the growth phase, but even freemium poses a risk if competitors come knocking too early. Netscape employed this strategy in the 1990s by offering its browser free for noncommercial use but charging corporate clients. That worked for a while with limited competition, but Microsoft eventually destroyed Netscape. Microsoft borrowed from the venture capital playbook and introduced its 100 percent free Internet Explorer. Then it further fueled growth by bundling the browser into almost every personal computer on the planet.

Microsoft is a rare example of an established company stealing customers from a venture start-up in a new market during the growth phase. More often than not, larger companies are hamstrung by their own success. Imagine being in the position where your company is making millions and you're faced with the opportunity of giving that money away to potentially win a new market. Most leaders aren't bold enough to take on that challenge, so they retrench and attempt to maintain their market position. For an individual CEO, that might be the right move. It ensures profits and reduces short-term risk. But over the long run, lack of innovation often leaves companies in a state of peril (of course, by that time the CEO is retired). This is one reason that even large companies rarely survive past 50 years or so.

To survive in a growth phase, you must own the market. That means putting aside profit, revenue opportunities, and anything else that could starve the network of needed oxygen. The goal is to consume all of the oxygen, which both allows your technology to grow and blocks any others from sprouting.

III

Anyone who drives in cities such as London, Los Angeles, or Atlanta must wonder why cities don't increase the size of the highway system to reduce traffic. The answer is that highways are networks, and this means that bigger is not always better. While size matters during the early development of a network, eventually it becomes a hindrance. Solving the traffic problem by adding more lanes is an urban myth; it doesn't really work. Writing in *The Atlantic*, Stephen Budiansky explained how scientists have observed "an interesting paradox about the flow of vehicular traffic." When engineers and city planners add new roads or lanes, under certain circumstances, they may actually reduce the whole traffic network's car-carrying capacity. "It turns out that the properties collectively exhibited by large numbers of cars moving over a network of roadways have many mathematical features in common with the behavior of other things that flow over networks, such as data carried by telephone lines and the Internet."

The internet, just like the brain, can use TCP to slow traffic when things get congested. But there really is no parallel for highways. Cities have tried all manner of ideas: adding lanes, creating tolls, adding ramp stoplights. Nothing has relieved congested highways during rush hours.

Recently, the city of Stockholm tried a novel approach to deal with its traffic congestion problems: they started charging drivers a tax when they drove on certain severely congested roads at certain times. This was the first time someone thought of taxing driving at specific times. The idea was conceived in part by Jonas Eliasson, professor of transportation at Stockholm's Royal Institute of Technology, and it was considered radical when first introduced. Most people in the community were violently against it. Yet it worked.

Almost overnight, there were 20 percent fewer cars during peak traffic hours. Twenty percent doesn't seem like a huge decrease; after all, 80 percent of the cars were still on the road, and in many cases these hotspots were at old, narrow bridges, as there is lots of water to cross in Stockholm. It turned out, however, that removing 20 percent of the cars resulted in alleviating 100 percent of the congestion. It also had the unintended effect of increasing air quality, as smog must be evenly distributed throughout the day to avoid build up. Dr. Eliasson explained it this way: "Traffic happens to be a nonlinear phenomenon, meaning that once you reach above a certain capacity threshold then congestion starts to increase really, really rapidly. But fortunately, it also works the other way around. If you can reduce traffic even somewhat, then congestion will go down much faster than you might think."

A city's network of roads has a natural breakpoint—a point where the road can no longer handle the number of cars without causing traffic backups. When that breakpoint is exceeded even a little, the roads go from flowing smoothly to massively congested in an instant. This is no surprise because we've seen the same phenomenon with biological networks, whether it be ants, reindeer, Easter Islanders, or the brain.

While the traffic change in Stockholm was dramatic, the psychological effects, or lack thereof, were equally profound. Despite the fact that people either had to pay or change their driving habits, few complained. More than that, few even noticed. Those who had to pay were happy to do so because there was less traffic, and surveys showed that those who changed their behavior didn't actually realize they had changed. The shift was so subtle that it went virtually unnoticed.

IV

Money is highly disruptive, even in small amounts. Against the backdrop of an overloaded network, money can be used to manipulate volume. For example, airlines constantly adjust ticket prices for air travel in order to keep the volume of travelers at the exact carrying capacity of their network. Too few travelers on an airplane and potential revenue is lost; too many travelers and the system is completely overloaded. Stockholm's congestion taxes were small amounts—between 0 and 20 SEK (1 SEK is roughly .10 Euros or .15 USD)—that had low economic impact for most, but the introduction of these costs created a disruption that changed the network dramatically.

Adding money into the equation *after* a breakpoint can serve two purposes: it can reduce congestion on a network filled to the brim, and it can help companies convert their valuable networks from free to revenue generating. The former can be used effectively right after a breakpoint, but the latter should be avoided until the network is more stable.

Take Facebook as an example. There are many places where the Facebook network has now exceeded capacity, and money could be used to curtail this. We learned how there are currently too many friend connections on the site to be valuable. What if Facebook charged users for additional friends above a certain number? It could be a nominal amount, perhaps a penny per extra friend. The impact would likely be similar to that in Stockholm after the congestion tax. Some users would happily pay for the extra connections, but many would naturally reduce their list of friends to a manageable number. The net effect would be reduced congestion and a more efficient and more powerful network. Interestingly, in 2013, Facebook experimented with a similar concept, introducing a pay-per-message system. It offered people who weren't friends with Mark Zuckerberg the chance to send him a message—for $100. The Zuckerberg fee was only an experiment, but it shows the extent to which Facebook is willing to charge users for communicating outside of their inner circles.

Turning a free network into a profit center is enticing but risky. Because Facebook is past its breakpoint, it could use this technique to make serious money, and the network could bear it. But smaller networks should be extremely careful. Networks that attempt to make money from their users before the breakpoint risk a complete collapse. Before it is exhausted, carrying capacity can ebb and flow, potentially leaving room for competitors. Charging too much for a feature that many users find valuable isn't smart.

The same is true with advertising. It should be well noted that very few successful networks allowed advertising from the beginning—it wasn't present on Google, Facebook, LinkedIn, or Twitter until the sites reached maturity. Even then, advertising was introduced slowly, and there were numerous times at which a company had to pull back certain programs.

Consider how Google began to make money. For the first few years, it didn't. There were no user charges and no ads. The company began toying with revenue models only after they hit scale but did nothing significant until 2000, when Google launched AdWords, a targeted advertising system unlike what was typical on the web. The ads were designed to act like content: they consisted of text that was relevant to the user's search. AdWords wasn't scaled until 2003 with the launch of a new technology called AdSense, at which point Google had largely beat out every other search engine. And from there, Google reaped the rewards, with revenues growing from a respectable $83 million in 2001 to almost $1.5 billion three years later. In 2012, Google's revenues were over $46 billion.

Facebook's dominance is as clear as Google's. They are well past the breakpoint, and users are more than willing to pay in terms of time, distractions, and cost. Unsurprisingly, Facebook has recently made a major push into advertising, with much of it being invasive, targeted, and highly personal. Facebook is using people's content, friends, and even their habits to sell products on behalf of advertisers. The lines have blurred to such an extent that in some cases it is hard to tell friendly content from ad content. Facebook has even converted comments from users into real ads. One user posted a joke about a personal lubricant and Facebook converted it into a Valentine's Day ad. But even at this extreme, users in a network past breakpoint are willing to put up with these tactics. The *New York Times* quoted the lubricated user as saying, "I was mildly annoyed, though not to the point of deleting my Facebook account or throwing a hissy fit."

Of course, not everyone can be Google or Facebook. But the point is that even these companies held off on making money before they had stable dominance across the internet. It is tempting to try monetization early, but the rewards for long-term patience are great.

The message is equally applicable to smaller companies. Often, small businesses cannot easily dominate a large market, nor do they have the resources to subsidize costs. The trick for a small business is to redefine the market so that it is small enough to own. Here again, Facebook provides a great example. When Facebook was launched in February 2004, MySpace was the dominant social network, and there was no hope for Facebook to compete. In a stroke of brilliance, Mark Zuckerberg limited his network to Harvard students. That allowed Facebook to dominate a much smaller market. Within a few months, half of Harvard's student body were Facebook users. Only after hitting a breakpoint at Harvard did Facebook open to students at other Ivy League schools. Slowly, it allowed all college students and then high school students to join. It took another three years before Facebook opened the network to the world. And perhaps most importantly, it was a total of five years before Facebook began making any money.

All businesses can learn from the Facebook story. For the largest businesses with the biggest goals, this "network of networks" approach is a great way to move into a market. If your sights are broad, first tackle a smaller market and then use that network dominance to move into other markets until you reach your ultimate goal.

A smaller business must focus on a market it can truly own. If Zuckerberg had been thinking small, he could have limited his network to Harvard and then quickly monetized to reap the rewards of a small but dominant network. That would have worked perfectly well, and his dominance at Harvard would likely still persist today. The idea for a small business is to focus on an appropriately sized market, geography, or category and dominate that niche. A company that has grown to lead the network for skydiving in Boise, Idaho, for example, can reap the rewards and make money. Networks of underwater basket weavers, fountain pen fanatics, or F-16 pilots can be equally vibrant.

There are countless success stories in this regard. Edmodo, created by two Illinois school district employees, is a site limited solely to teachers and their students. It's both a social network and a virtual classroom. The *Huffington Post* reported that over 25 percent of all teachers—inside and outside of Illinois—are already using the site, which is replacing more general social networks for teachers and students. That number is up from 3 percent penetration only a few years ago. Once Edmodo fully dominates the market, the network will be extremely valuable, though admittedly smaller than Facebook or Twitter.

Businesses don't have to create their own network to benefit from network dominance. Most businesses aren't in the network-creation business, but almost all can leverage other networks. Naked Pizza used Twitter to build its business and expand into markets outside of its native New Orleans. The business collected followers market by market; once Naked Pizza had critical mass in a given market, they opened a store and used the network to generate excitement in their customer base. *Entrepreneur* magazine noted that the buzz for Naked Pizza was disproportionate to its size, and the *New York Times* highlighted Naked Pizza as one of 11 companies whose Twitter strategies should be emulated. The company's founders perhaps stated it best when they explained that rather than running a pizza company, they are actually "running a social media operation that happens to sell pizza."

The benefits of a stable network are worth the wait for companies large and small. Stable networks are no longer at risk of losing users. Users will come and go, just as neurons come and go in the brain. But the larger network will remain intact. Economists call these "natural monopolies," a term originally coined by John Stuart Mill. A natural monopoly occurs when it is most efficient for an entire market to be represented by a single company. You often see these monopolies in a utility industry, for example, but they also exist within networks. This is because in both cases, the value of an additional user is disproportionally greater than typical economies of scale. In these industries, user growth provides higher value to a single company than it would to multiple companies.

What business doesn't want to be on the right side of a monopoly? Markets change, and that shift can cause a decline, but otherwise natural monopolies will persist in networks. (Of course, sometimes the government can get involved, which is always a concern. AT&T found this out in the 1980s, when the US government forced it to split because of its domination of the telephone network.) Nonetheless, the benefit of waiting until your network is dominant cannot be overstated.

LinkedIn, which recently surpassed 200 million users, has had considerable success navigating these waters. The site targets professionals and LinkedIn has done an impressive job of staying true to that niche. They have never encouraged users to add sparse connections; in fact, the site doesn't allow people to see that you have a million connections (it will show "500+" in that case). This eliminates the popularity contests that abounded on MySpace and persist on Facebook. LinkedIn highlights degrees of separation, letting users know just how connected two people are.

LinkedIn also employs a freemium model, where the site is generally free to use but requires a subscription to access certain features. It charges users who want to dig deeper into the network. The pay features tend to be higher level, so there is no real risk of average users feeling slighted. The company does take advantage of advertising, but here, too, LinkedIn's cycle followed the right path: it started ad-free, later employed content-rich, non-invasive ads, and only recently started displaying more prominent ads.

It shouldn't surprise us that LinkedIn figured out a successful strategy, as the company was founded and led by one of the most prolific networking investors of our day, Reid Hoffman. Hoffman has invested in virtually every network imaginable and has likely seen the stages across each of them. Hoffman's list is almost too long, but it includes early adopters and powerhouses alike, including SocialNet, PayPal, Facebook, Zynga, Wikia, Digg, SixApart, and Last.fm. Without a playbook for how networks unfold, the next best thing is to witness how it happens across a few dozen successes and failures.

With so much focus on growth, few people have seen what happens to networks in the long term. Growth is necessary when oxygen remains, but once it runs out, you have hit the breakpoint. At this stage, the carrying capacity has been consumed and the market is dominated. It is then, when it is almost impossible for formidable competition to arise, that there is an opportunity for a network to become a business. A network past its breakpoint is like a sea squirt who has found his lasting rock home: it's time to reap the rewards and eat the brain.

NINE

PHEROMONES | LANGUAGE | MIRRORS

D espite their minimal brainpower and inability to speak, ants are remarkably good at communicating, which they do automatically through scent. Their bodies are covered in a greasy layer called cuticular hydrocarbon, and each ant carries a unique cuticular hydrocarbon pheromone, or scent, that is specific to the colony. When an ant encounters another ant, she touches her antennae to the other ant's antennae or body, and she can instantly determine whether the ant is part of her own colony. If she finds that the other ant is a nestmate, she investigates further and can smell where the ant has been, what task the ant is currently performing, and, in some cases, what the ant has eaten recently.

Ants come in contact with many nestmates throughout the course of the day. The patterns of a particular ant's interactions largely determine what task, if any, she decides to perform. When foraging, an ant follows scent trails left by other ants to know which direction to go and to predict how good the food will be.

When ants encounter high-quality food, they leave a stronger scent trail, thus encouraging other ants to follow the same trail and bring back more of the good stuff.

Ants have a much more acute sense of smell than do other insects. A new study by biologist Laurence Zwiebel at Vanderbilt University mapped out a typical ant olfactory system and found that they have 400 different olfactory receptors. This is a huge number for an insect; honeybees have fewer than 200, and fruit flies have a paltry 61 of these odor-detecting proteins. "It's a reasonable supposition," says Dr. Zwiebel, "that this dramatic expansion in odor-sensing capability is what allowed ants to develop such a high level of social organization."

The nuances of scent are vital to the survival of ant colonies. In fact, if you want to fool an ant colony, all you have to do is have the right scent. One type of jumping spider has evolved a unique survival strategy: they copy the scent of a particular colony and walk right into the nest. They steal larvae right under the ants' noses, which don't detect intruders that have replicated the colony scent.

Perhaps most interesting to study are the interactions between ants from different colonies. Most often, they avoid each other at all costs. As Deborah Gordon puts it, "Ants sometimes look like they jump apart after an encounter with an ant that is not a nestmate, recoiling from the unfamiliar smell." If a harvester ant meets ants from a different colony while foraging, she heads in the other direction immediately. She does not lay down a scent trail on her way home, which keeps other nestmates from heading in the direction of the foreign ants.

Harvester ants generally don't fight, but "there seem to be seasonal bursts of fighting, often just after the summer rains," says Dr. Gordon. "Maybe the rain washes away chemical signals on the ground, such as colony-specific cuticular hydrocarbons, and the absence of those signals stimulates fighting." So it seems that while ants avoid foreign-smelling ants, the absence of scent creates all sorts of mayhem.

Ant networks require robust and precise communication, and evolution has outfitted ants with the necessary organs both to receive communication—their 400 olfactory receptors—and to "speak" their own language—through an amalgamation of glands on various body parts including the rectum, sternum, and hind tibia. Thus equipped, ants within a colony speak fluently to each other. Outside of the colony, however, communication breaks down.

So it is with humans. We tend to understand best those who speak the same language. Of course, even that general statement isn't true without certain caveats. Flawless communication is a rarity because language is subject to many complex factors, including age, education level, and geography. Many an American tourist in London has found that George Bernard Shaw was correct in his assessment that America and Britain are two nations divided by a common language. Closer to home, parents lament that their teenage sons and daughters speak a completely different—and often completely unintelligible—language.

We forge stronger connections with those with whom we communicate best. Our most important personal networks are made up of people who "get" us, and a large portion of that designation is determined by how well they speak our unique language.

To be sure, the internet has broken down countless barriers between people who speak different languages. It's a truly universal platform, enabling us to understand people a world away in terms of both distance and experience. The underlying process is remarkable. To exchange thoughts with a colleague in Japan, an

American professor must first input his thoughts in English into the computer through his fingers. These thoughts then go through the web (different language), then across the internet (different language), only to be translated and displayed in Japanese (different language). Currently the internet attempts to make sense of 8,512 computer languages, dozens of HTML-based web languages, and nearly 6,500 active spoken human languages. But we're not there yet.

No network—ant, human, or technological—can achieve maximum success without efficient communication. The internet will not reach its full potential until we find a way to overcome the language barrier. Though the network is already solid, it will become infinitely stronger once we figure out how to coat ourselves—all of us—in the same cuticular hydrocarbons. In order for the internet to evolve, it has to learn to communicate, just as ants did millions of years ago and humans did thousands of years ago.

|

Most people have never met a linguist in real life and assume they must be something on the order of Noam Chomsky, a quixotic character from MIT in a tweed jacket who has the nasty habit of correcting elocution in public. You wouldn't want to sit next to one at a dinner party. But at the risk of overstating the case, linguists today have become the Indiana Joneses of brain science—great explorers of the unknown.

The previously stodgy world of linguistics has become a hotbed of innovation. In fact, almost every large internet company now employs linguists, and there is an army of them across the web. "Until recently, linguistics was mainly an academic pursuit and those jobs were hard to get and not that well-paying," said Ed

Stabler, associate professor of computational linguistics at UCLA. "Now—in spite of university offers—almost all of my PhDs are in the dot-com industry. In the past five years, the change has been phenomenal."

Language underlies many of the technologies that make the internet useful to all of us. Take search engines, for example. Google deploys intelligent software to "read" a website, and that's how it matches the best webpages to a search keyword. At this very moment, Google and the other search engines are actively reading thousands of websites to determine their relevance to various user searches. Words, after all, are the fundamental unit of human intelligence, and language is the foundation of civilization. Sigmund Freud had it right when he said, "The first human who hurled an insult instead of a stone was the founder of civilization."

Speaking in words is a uniquely human accomplishment, something that no other animal or computer has mastered. For linguists, the study of language, grammar, and the logic and reason implicit within is the key that unlocks the secrets of the mind. Language is enlightening not only because it allows us insight into how we perceive the world, but also because it indicates how we retrieve information. The ways in which we structure words into sentences and sentences into paragraphs reveal the logic behind our thoughts. And, of course, they reveal the continuous illogic that makes human beings human. Google and the other Silicon Valley companies hiring Professor Stabler's students are attempting to leverage the power of language to turn the internet into a thinking, reasoning brain. But there is a catch: language acquisition happens in the brain before the breakpoint, and it is likely that the same will be true of the internet. This is the primary reason that so many companies are rushing to hire linguists—they see the opportunity but they also know it may slip away.

II

Linguists have learned that there is a critical developmental period when it is easiest for a child to acquire a first language. This concept was first raised theoretically in 1959 by McGill University neurologist Wilder Penfield, and subsequent research has provided confirmation. While scholars disagree on some of the specifics, it is generally accepted that the critical period for learning a primary language is from the age of 4 months until roughly age 5. After that time, it is very difficult to learn a first language. (It is believed that another critical period exists for the learning of second languages. This stage ends roughly at puberty, at which time language acquisition in general becomes far more difficult.)

It is largely believed that the reason for the critical period is that the brain is far more plastic during the growth phase than it is beyond the breakpoint. When neural connections are growing, the brain remains highly adaptive, which encourages learning. As those connections dissipate, the brain becomes more highly tuned but also more rigid. As a result, it is far easier for a child to acquire language, which requires flexible neurons that can learn and adapt. Later in life, language acquisition is more difficult because the neurons are more fixed.

An alternative theory is equally plausible: after the brain's breakpoint, we may actually lose many of the neural connections necessary to encode language. Once the brain has acquired a primary language, there is no need to carry those costly networks with us, as there is little evolutionary benefit to having multiple languages. Harvard linguist Steven Pinker provides an eloquent argument for this theory in *The Language Instinct*: "Language acquisition circuitry is not needed once it has been used. It should be dismantled if keeping it around incurs any cost . . . Greedy neural tissue lying around beyond its point of usefulness is a good candidate for the recycling bin."

Regardless of which theory is correct, it is now clear that language learning has its own breakpoint, which is distinguished from the network stages of the brain. As University of Texas language professor David Birdsong makes clear of language acquisition, "Typically, there is an abrupt onset or increase of sensitivity, a plateau of peak sensitivity, followed by a gradual offset or decline, with subsequent flattening of the degree of sensitivity." In other words, there is a growth phase, a breakpoint, and then a period of equilibrium, as Birdsong illustrated.

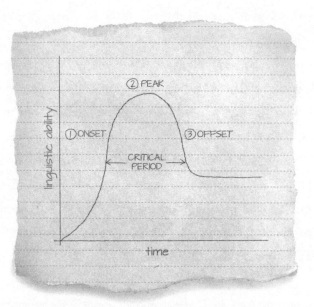

Image 9.1: The Critical Period in Language Acquisition

|||

Learning language is not as easy as merely learning words. As Steven Pinker notes, "If there is a bag in your car, and a gallon of milk in the bag, there is a gallon of milk in your car. But if there's a person in your car, and a gallon of blood in a person, it would be strange to conclude that there is a gallon of blood in your car." It might take the hundred billion neurons residing in your cerebral cortex a second or two to figure that out. But chances are good that no computer today, regardless of its vaulted silicon IQ, would understand. These are the kind of language and thinking cues that the internet must pick up on. Otherwise, for all of its ability to make calculations a million times faster than the neurons in a brain, the internet will be horribly ineffectual.

Linguists weren't always interested in the internet, and until recently, internet companies similarly ignored the field of linguistics. Despite the internet's dependence on words, the general consensus was that it was just too difficult to tie words to meanings. But that all changed with a single innovation developed at Princeton by the late renowned psychologist George Miller. Miller's innovation was something called WordNet, created in 1985 and perfected over the following 15 years. By the turn of the century, the principles of WordNet were in use across the internet, spurring the need for legions of linguists. For his part, Miller won dozens of awards, including the National Medal of Science from the White House.

WordNet was a bold attempt to categorize and store human language in computers in a way similar to the way the brain stores language. Consider the following:

vehicle → motor vehicle → automobile = auto = car → sports car
→ Porsche → 911, 944, Boxster, Cayenne, Cayman, Panamera

Almost every word in natural language has both generalizations and specializations of this kind. These relationships form a network structure that sits on top of our neurons in our memory systems. The power of this type of network representation is that it puts specific information in a more general framework that can be used to compute answers to queries.

This is great news for search engines. Without WordNet, when a user types in "Boxster," all that can be searched is "Boxster." But with a network structure like WordNet, search engines can also activate the "sports car" and "Porsche" nodes, which elicit even more robust information. The user can quickly discover that Boxsters have high-powered engines, usually seat two people, and aren't exactly cheap. Word networks are also powerful tools for spell checkers and thesauruses, allowing—among other things— the autocorrect function on your emails to act smarter based on the context of what is being written. It also solves the problem of context for technologies like Apple's Siri, which tries to understand natural language.

Of course, there is an even bigger problem with language, namely, that words are ambiguous. If words used in natural language had single, well-defined meanings, life would be simple. Unfortunately, that is not the case. 911, as an example, has many meanings. Outside of being a type of sports car, it also conjures up images of September 11 specifically and emergencies in general. Language is a complex, ever-evolving instrument: a quick look at a dictionary will show that essentially all common words have multiple meanings. In fact, the more frequently a word is used, the more meanings it is likely to have. To complicate things further, it is a truism in linguistics that each word means something at least slightly different, so even synonyms are never really true equals.

Consider the two words "board" and "plank." Both can refer to pieces of wood. The two statements, "He went to Home Depot and purchased a knotty pine *board*" and "He went to Home Depot and purchased a knotty pine *plank*," mean about the same thing. However, both "board" and "plank" have multiple meanings, and these other meanings are completely different. For example, "board" and "plank" are not interchangeable in the following sentence: "The venture capitalist will throw the CEO off a *plank* if he is not elected to the *board* of the corporation."

We humans deal with this very well. As an example, when someone hears the three words "bat, ball, diamond," she knows the topic is almost surely related to baseball, even though all the words in the string are ambiguous. "Bat" could refer to a flying mammal or a wooden club, "diamond" to a gem or a shape, and "ball" to a dance or a sphere. The common association of the words in the string, "baseball," is obvious given the context of our language network.

It's generally effortless for a reasonably intelligent person to choose the right meaning based on context, even when a word has many possible meanings. However, this problem is so difficult for computers that it stopped early attempts at artificial intelligence dead in their tracks. A word is surrounded by an invisible cloud of context and world knowledge that is tapped easily by humans but largely unavailable to computers.

WordNet deals with multiple word meanings by the formation of what Miller called "synsets," that is, sets of synonyms. Each synset consists of groups of words that share a particular meaning; they act as synonyms, but only for a single meaning. To follow up on the previous example, "board" and "plank" form a synset when referring to the meaning "pieces of wood."

However, both "board" and "plank" have other meanings that are not shared.

WordNet uses a brain science algorithm called "spreading activation" to solve the problem of ambiguity. Spreading activation is a process by which closely connected words wire and fire together, just like neurons. One word activates others nearby in the network. Consider again a bat, a ball, and a diamond. Each word has multiple meanings. Yet each word contains a meaning linked to baseball among its sets of meanings. If we simply excite links connected to each meaning, the "baseball" node will get three times as much excitation as the meanings that are not common to all the words. Spreading activation thus solves the meaning problem: when someone says bat, ball, and diamond, WordNet can tell that baseball is involved (rather than flying mammals or weddings). In this way, WordNet approximates semantic maps with synsets that allow the internet to build context into language through spreading activation.

For a more practical example, consider someone who needs to buy a new outfit. He may search for shirts, pants, shoes, jackets, and socks. Clothing is the unifying category. If each of these specific terms "spreads" activation to parts of the network connected to it, "clothing" will be activated multiple times, once from each subordinate. Such a computation is immeasurably valuable in e-commerce because we know that shirts are rarely sold in "shirt stores" or pants in "pants stores," but both are found in clothing stores. Knowing the right level of generality needed is a matter of great importance and is often difficult for computers to determine without help. WordNet provides the key.

Without this intelligence, companies across the web are prone to make the same comical errors we expect from children. It brings to mind the first version of Google's advertising system, which inadvertently placed a luggage ad on a news article describing how a woman was murdered and stuffed into a suitcase. Google went on to buy a company leveraging George Miller's WordNet and incorporated it into their advertising system. Virtually all search engines, and many advertising systems, now use some of these techniques to make their engines and algorithms "smart."

IV

Until the early 1990s, it was thought that all neurons worked the same way. They acted as simple processing units that fired as a result of specific stimuli. But in 1991, an amazing discovery happened that has fundamentally changed how we think about the brain.

Giacomo Rizzollati, a physiologist working at the University of Parma in Italy, was studying how neurons reacted when monkeys reached for and grasped objects. Rizzollati implanted electrodes into a monkey's brain and watched as the neurons predictably fired each time the monkey grasped a handful of nuts. This was nothing new or exciting: Rizzollati was studying processes that neuroscientists had long since confirmed. The body moves in response to the neurons in the motor cortex.

But then something unexpected happened: a graduate student walked into the lab with an ice cream cone. The monkey shifted his attention and watched as the student began to eat the ice cream . . . and the monkey's motor neurons became active.

Based on what we knew at the time, this result was just not possible. Individual neurons are supposed to perform single, simple functions. They are insular; motor neurons fire with our own motor movements, not the actions of someone else. And most importantly, they can't track our actions *and* the actions of others—it just doesn't work that way. It would be as if a car responded not just to the pressure of your foot on the gas pedal but also to that of the driver across the street in a different car. The result, in both cases, would be a crash.

As a neuroscientist, Rizzollati understood this as much as anyone. His first conclusion was simply that his gear was broken or that the neurons were connected improperly. So he tested other machines, other monkeys, other brain regions. In each case, he found the same result: neurons firing in response to the actions of others. Rizzollati had found a new type of neuron, now referred to as mirror neurons. (Interestingly, for his efforts, Rizzollati went on to win a prestigious award from the Cognitive Neuroscience Society named after George Miller, the creator of WordNet.)

Over the past ten years, other neuroscientists have duplicated Rizzollati's results and also demonstrated that these neurons exist in humans. Mirror neurons are truly remarkable and are redefining how we think about the brain. They are especially pronounced in humans; it is argued that we have far more mirror neurons—and that they are more complex—than do any other animals. Neuroscientists now believe that mirror neurons are responsible for much of our cognitive ability, especially in areas of empathy, culture, and language. The always-bold neuroscientist V. S. Ramachandran has gone so far as to predict that "mirror neurons will do for psychology what DNA did for biology."

Mirror neurons are not homunculi, nor are they intelligent. But they do something other neurons cannot do: make predictions. Mirror neurons in the motor cortex are able to predict the intention of an action (holding an ice cream cone versus eating it). Somehow, they fire only with the true intent; they don't respond to meaningless actions or random gestures. University of Southern California neuroscientist Michael Arbib places the mirror neuron into its full context: "The neurons, located in the premotor cortex just in front of the motor cortex, are a mechanism for recognizing the meaning of actions made by others."

But mirror neurons do even more than that. Found throughout the brain, they connect disparate themes with disparate pieces of information, allowing us to literally connect the dots. We see someone eating ice cream and motor mirror neurons fire. While that doesn't activate the motor cortex or cause us to mimic the action, it does seem to elicit responses from other areas of the brain, effectively connecting someone else's actions to our brains. Mirror neurons predict the actions of others, give us empathy, and place other people into the context of our lives.

Whereas WordNet demonstrated how we connect words to meanings, mirror neurons provided the necessary components to actually acquire language. It turns out that words are only a piece of the puzzle of language; the remainder comes from being able to make predictions. Scientists searching for insight into how we acquire language may have found their answer in mirror neurons.

Infants as young as a few weeks old begin mimicking the people around them. But so do birds, chimps, and even dogs. They move their mouths and tongues as others speak; they move their arms and legs as others walk; they move their heads and eyes in concert with others; they smile or frown in reaction to the expressions of others. This behavior is largely automatic; it's pure mimicry, not backed by intention or meaning.

But eventually toddlers begin to seek purpose. They start with mindless mimicking, but as the brain develops, mimicking turns to understanding. In this way, they can learn a language. This likely happens as a result of the development of mirror neurons in early childhood, during the brain's growth phase as it approaches its breakpoint. Once developed, mirror neurons fire in the brain when a complex pattern emerges. Mirror neurons connect language and motor areas of the brain, intricately linking actions (speech, writing, gestures, signing) to intentions.

It should be noted that mirror neurons were first found in monkeys even though they cannot speak. Because the mirror neurons of primates are primitive in comparison to those of humans, they cannot form as many meaningful connections. In turn, this limits their ability to develop complex language. In its place, primates communicate in rudimentary ways, using mirror neurons for making predictions about their environment rather than about the intentions of others.

V

Technology is devoid of mirrors. Robots, computers, and even the internet are stiff, predictable, and unemotional. The main reason for this is that we have thought of the job of machines as being mechanical, not emotional. In many ways, we have a dualistic approach: the computer can be a brain, but the mind is something different. As a result of this line of thinking, we have missed a wealth of opportunity.

Our attempts at reverse engineering the brain to build better computers led us to neurons, which we thought were logical. We now know that's not an accurate description, as neurons are quite fallible. Mirror neurons, however, are something different entirely: there is no real logic because they are constantly interpreting, guessing, and making predictions. We have always linked language to ideas and ideas to wisdom, but really it is our ability to predict that gives us our intelligence. In addition to language, the ability to predict comes from mirror neurons. Mirror neurons place our thoughts and actions into context and give us the ability to anticipate. It is that last ability that gives us wisdom.

It's ironic that our somewhat erratic, illogical decision making actually makes us wise. In *The Wisdom Paradox,* neuroscientist Elkhonon Goldberg describes the feeling of decision making: "As I am trying to solve a thorny problem," he writes, "a seemingly distant association often pops up like a *deus ex machina,* unrelated at first glance but in the end offering a marvelously effective solution to the problem at hand. Things that in the past were separate now reveal their connection. This, too, happens effortlessly, by itself, while I experience myself more as a passive recipient of a mental windfall than as an active straining agent of my mental life." Goldberg calls this wisdom and finds that as he ages—to his delight—he has more of it than when he was young. "What I have lost with age in my capacity for hard mental work, I seem to have gained in my capacity for instantaneous, almost unfairly easy insight."

Goldberg's mind is not a calculating machine, but it has developed associations, memories, emotions, and a *mechanism of anticipation* that actually raises the total beyond the sum of its parts. We call this wisdom, and it's not an out-of-the-brain phenomenon; it is a product of the brain. It is likely the work of the brain's mirror neurons.

To figure out what to do at any given moment, the brain must gaze into the future and imagine. The brain studies its environment, watches what others are doing, and simulates possible future scenarios. Then the brain evaluates those scenarios to guess which are most likely. And then, to save energy (so that it doesn't have to interpret, calculate, and guess again and again), it learns from those simulations. Ultimately, the thought surfaces, not in the past, not in the present, but in the future tense: "What next?"

Forward thinking is the brain's way of chipping away at the edges of uncertainty. It makes bets based on past experiences. The human brain learns and remembers not only what happened, but also what didn't happen. And it turns the sum of this disconnected, limited information into real insight. As Pinker notes, we make "fallible guesses from fragmentary information."

VI

Some of the most innovative technology companies have found ways to leverage our prediction capabilities. Netflix, for example, created a technology called Cinematch that helps its customers find movies. Netflix takes a customer's previously watched movies and, with some fancy algorithmic gymnastics, matches them against thousands of other possible films. (Netflix refers to what it does as "straightforward statistical linear modeling, with a lot of data conditioning.") Thanks to the Cinematch algorithms, Netflix can even recommend the perfect "movie for two," which, considering the Venus-Mars tastes of many couples, should be considered a minor miracle. The algorithm works because it takes vast amounts of information, makes predictions, and learns from those predictions.

But Cinematch is not without its problems. In the past, one of its largest weaknesses was that its algorithms tended to recommend only best sellers. Because of this, many outlying films, those that might really surprise and please particular viewers, were ignored. This was not a problem Netflix knew how to solve, so they offered a million dollars to anyone who could improve Cinematch by at least 10 percent.

With that, the crowdsourced Netflix Prize discussed in chapter 7 was born. Within months, some 25,000 teams and individuals applied for the Netflix Prize and were given a set of 100 million ratings of over 17,000 movies. After three years, two teams were finally able to make a 10 percent improvement in the recommendations. Admirable, but Netflix is still not as good as a friend at making recommendations. In fact, Netflix never actually used the winning algorithms. By the time the award was given, Netflix had realized that the logical approach was not good enough. Many experts, such as MIT's Devavrat Shah, continue to criticize Netflix for its poor recommendations.

The problem stems from the fact that neither Netflix nor the competing teams were looking at the right data. In many ways, they were swimming in too much data and suffering from information overload. Netflix has several billion recommendations, with millions of new ones coming in every single day. Just like the field of artificial intelligence, Netflix's approach was to take a mound of data and try to analyze it. The Netflix algorithm team truly believed that "more data availability enables better results." They had all of the logical information they thought they needed, but logical information failed to provide perfect recommendations for illogical humans.

Netflix was missing the psychological data, what marketers call psychographics, the warm and fuzzy information that doesn't fit well into a model. This type of data enables empathy, insight, and an understanding of individuals and their choices. In other words, it allows the system to act as a network of mirror neurons. No one was surprised when, after the announcement of the first winners, Netflix CEO Reed Hastings announced a new Netflix Prize, but this time Netflix made available much of the needed psychological and contextual data.

While Netflix has worked hard to create a savvy recommendation technology, Amazon.com holds the prize for the most sophisticated prediction system. They use this system broadly, making suggestions for products that are bought together, items that others purchase, and personalized deals they call "Quick Picks." They even have a technology called a "Betterizer," which gives users the ability to improve their own recommendations. Many analysts credit Amazon's success—in 2012 they had over $61 billion in revenues—to these sophisticated predictions. Forrester Research estimated that as much as 60 percent of Amazon's recommendations turn into sales.

In many ways, Amazon's system is successful because it discards obvious logical data in favor of looking for behavioral patterns. In an approach that mirrors WordNet, Amazon uses something called "item-to-item collaborative filtering." This type of collaborative filtering essentially means that for each product, Amazon builds a synset of related products. Whenever someone views a product or makes a purchase, Amazon can use spreading activation to recommend items from that product's synset. Amazon's engineers described it as follows: "Given a similar-items table, the algorithm finds items similar to each of the user's purchases and ratings, aggregates those items, and then recommends the most popular or correlated items . . . Because the algorithm recommends highly correlated similar items, recommendation quality is excellent."

But the twist is that Amazon creates its similar-items table not by looking at the characteristics of the products but by looking at purchase behavior. If you buy a food processor, Amazon doesn't just recommend a blender because it's similar. Instead, it compares your purchase to those of other people who also bought the food processor to see what they would recommend— possibly batteries, an extension cord, or even a sponge to clean up the inevitable mess.

This is virtually identical to WordNet, except that instead of synsets that represent meanings, Amazon looks at the relationships between people's buying behavior, a type of psychographic. The formula relies on the overlap of different customers' purchases and recommendations. The results are often remarkably good because of algorithms that use humanlike decision making based on only a few pieces of psychological data. *Fortune* magazine had this to say about Amazon in 2012: "Much is made of what the likes of Facebook, Google and Apple know about users. Truth is, Amazon may know more." The irony is that Amazon knows more by using less. They take a simple approach, just like the brain, and ignore much of the extraneous information. Amazon's recommendation technology is so good that YouTube recently switched algorithms to a variation of Amazon's technology.

Often, Amazon's prediction algorithms result in recommendations that appear random but are, in fact, incredibly prescient. As Amazon founder and CEO Jeff Bezos puts it, "I remember one of the first times this struck me. The main book on the page was on Zen. There were other suggestions for Zen books, and in the middle of those was a book on how to have a clutter-free desk." Bezos goes on to say that this is not something a human would do.

But Bezos is mistaken: this is exactly the type of thing a human would do, and that is what makes it so powerful. Amazon was able to make the link between a Zen book, past behavior, and the fact that Bezos was looking to clean up his desk, just as a colleague might do after peering through a stack of papers only to find a hapless coworker feverishly purchasing a book on Zen.

Where Bezos is right, however, is that Amazon is missing an analogue to mirror neurons, and that limits its overall abilities. Most recommendation engines, including those of Amazon and

Netflix, use something far more similar to WordNet, where they look for meaning and context by comparing one group to another. It works to some extent, but eventually a mirror equivalent will provide better, more nuanced predictions.

Mirror neurons are on the way for both companies. Netflix has recently started using data from social networks. Leveraging a network of friends to make recommendations is the perfect way to gain insight through mirrors. Imagine the power of having movie recommendations from friends on Facebook or the people you follow on Twitter. For its part, Amazon has been quietly using mirror neurons for years. Their email system has a unique recommendation engine that dates back 200,000 years: humans. Marketing emails don't need to be quick or automated, so Amazon has its employees personally make recommendations to targeted groups. Perhaps this is cheating in technological terms, but it works wonders. Both Netflix and Amazon have realized that to provide the most valuable recommendations and true personalization, it is critical to understand intent and speak the language of their users.

VII

We still haven't solved the fundamental problem of true language understanding. While we've broken down numerous barriers with previous technological revolutions, the seemingly simple task of language translation still eludes us. We have made progress, but language is still a core problem on the internet. Many scientists, scholars, and entrepreneurs are working to bridge this gap.

Scientists have attempted to fix the language problem in three general ways. The first proposed solution is the creation of a single universal language. But this solution hasn't gained much traction because it's politically untenable. Americans aren't going to give up English, let alone the Brits, and there would be mutiny altogether in France over an attempt to abolish French. Equally important, it is difficult for people to learn new languages after the critical language period, so we would strand most adults. As eloquently simple as it may sound, creating a new universal language is impractical.

The second approach is one that many people in the field of linguistics are working on: language translation. Linguistics labs all over the world are abuzz trying to figure out how to translate and map disparate languages. The problem, though, is that translation is much more difficult than it seems. Language is a dynamic system, evolving as we evolve. Even if you could create a perfect translation system, by the time it was complete, the languages would have changed. This is not unlike the creation of dictionaries, which tend to be outdated mere weeks after publication. The difference is that with translation, the problem is compounded because there are multiple languages involved. There are also cultural dialect issues and more difficult problems like dealing with slang.

A third approach, however, shows real promise. No surprise, it stems from the brain. Communication within the mind uses electricity, specifically electrical neuronal spikes. That language underlies all language. And we know what it sounds like: neuronal spikes sound like crackling static, similar to what you hear when the radio searches for a signal. This is the fundamental building block of language. If we can take this neuronal spike and map it to the fundamental building block for how the internet and computers communicate, we will have an opportunity to make translations at the root level of thought. And there is reason to believe that this is possible. Computers and transistors communicate using the same electrical currents that neurons do. If you listen to them, they have identical voices. This begs an important question: If the internet and the brain are functionally the same, and if they communicate in the exact same way, why can't they speak to one another? When we are able to solve this problem, there will be a new network revolution afoot.

TEN

EEG | ESP | AI

O ver the past two million years, the human brain has been growing steadily. But something has recently changed. In a surprising reversal, human brains have been shrinking for the last 20,000 years or so. We have lost nearly a baseball-sized amount of matter from a brain that isn't any larger than a football. The descent is rapid and pronounced. Anthropologist John Hawks describes it as a "major downsizing in an evolutionary eyeblink." If this pace is maintained, scientists predict that our brains will be no larger than those of our forebears, *Homo erectus*, within another 2,000 years.

This finding is very different from what happens at the brain's breakpoint, where it loses some neurons and connections. In this case, the brain loss is an overall shrinking of our species' collective brains, and it means that individual brains have less to work with from the beginning. This isn't an evolutionary equilibrium, and it's not an efficiency trick to enable greater intelligence.

One reason that our brains are shrinking is that we are physically smaller than our burly ape ancestors. Remember, brain size is directly proportional to body mass—bigger bodies generally need bigger brains for movement. But that only accounts for a tiny amount of the brain loss, maybe the size of a pea. Brain scientist David Geary has a more alarming answer: "You may not want to hear this, but I think the best explanation for the decline in our brain size is the idiocracy theory." In other words, we are getting dumber.

Many of the evolutionary traits we think of as beneficial are not really that critical. We assume that everywhere in the animal kingdom, the evolution of intelligence is important. It is not. Evolution is not concerned with progress, only with survival. Certainly, intelligence is hugely important to some species. But brains are costly in terms of weight and energy, so greater intelligence is often more dangerous than beneficial. For animals like birds, for instance, flight would not be possible with larger, heavier brains.

The reason that our brains are shrinking is simple: our biology is focused on survival, not intelligence. Larger brains were necessary to allow us to learn to use language, tools, and all of the innovations that allowed our species to thrive. But now that we have become civilized—domesticated, if you will—our brains are less necessary. This is actually true of all animals: domesticated animals, including dogs, cats, hamsters, and birds, have 10 to 15 percent smaller brains than their counterparts in the wild. Because brains are so expensive to maintain, large brain sizes are selected out when Mother Nature sees no direct survival benefit. It is a true and inevitable fact of life.

|

It is daunting to imagine a time when we will not be the brains we once were, but there is no need to fear. Another influence has evolved over the past 20,000 years that is making us smarter even as our brains are shrinking: technology. Technology has allowed us to leapfrog evolution, enabling our brains and bodies to do things that were otherwise impossible biologically. We weren't born with wings, but we've enabled flight by creating airplanes, helicopters, hot air balloons, and hang gliders. We don't have sufficient natural strength or speed to bring down big game, but we've created spears, rifles, and livestock farms.

We are not only extending our natural abilities, we are doing so with increasing speed and efficiency as technology gets better, faster, and cheaper. We've improved our world in revolutionary stages. Our first major coup, back in the cradle of civilization, was climbing down from the trees. This simple act changed us permanently and placed our species on a trajectory of rapid growth. By moving to a biped world, we were able to do all kinds of things that were previously out of reach. In short order we created things like the wheel and fire.

Next came the agricultural revolution. This transformation enabled us to spread out geographically and lay deep roots. We learned to plant and cultivate crops; we centered our lives on farming. Perhaps the single most important human innovation—culture—formed as a result.

Fast-forward to the advent of the printing press and its accompanying print revolution. For the first time in history, we were able to spread ideas far and wide through books. No longer bound by the geography of storytellers, books enabled us to ship ideas off on a boat to the other side of the world. And the ideas were perfectly recorded; they didn't change with each iteration as in a game of telephone. As a result of printing, we also became able to transport our ideas across time. Our books preserve our stories and ideas generation after generation.

The industrial revolution brought us a mechanized world. With this leap forward, humanity experienced a fourfold increase in population and a twofold increase in quality of life and wealth. Never before or since has something like this happened. The mechanized world transformed us, increasing our efficiency and carrying capacity in one fell swoop.

The digital revolution came not long after. While prior innovations extended our bodies, the advent of computers expanded our minds. Where we are limited in logical thinking, computers can calculate perfectly. Where we are limited in memory, computers can store infinite information.

The innovations that fascinate me most come from the internet revolution. We are seeing here not merely an extension of mind but a unity of mind and machine, two networks coming together as one. We have learned about the brain and are now using that knowledge to create new technology. Our smaller, more efficient brains are in a quest to bypass nature's intent and grow larger by proxy.

II

In the late 1800s, German astronomer Hans Berger fell off a horse and was nearly trampled by a cavalry. He narrowly escaped injury but was forever changed by the incident owing to the reaction of his sister. Though she was miles away at the time, Berger's sister became instantly overcome with a feeling that Hans was in trouble. Berger took this as evidence of the mind's psychic ability and dedicated the rest of his life to finding certain proof.

Berger abandoned his study of astronomy and enrolled in medical school to gain an understanding of the brain that would allow him to prove a "correlation between objective activity in the brain and subjective psychic phenomena." He later joined the University of Jena in Germany as professor of neurology to pursue his quest.

At the time, psychic interest was relatively high. There were numerous academics devoted to the field, studying at prestigious institutions such as Stanford and Duke in the US and Oxford and Cambridge in the UK. Still, it was largely considered bunk science, with most credible academics focused on dispelling, rather than proving, myths of psychic ability. But one of those psychic beliefs happened to be true.

That belief is the now understood notion that our brains communicate electrically. This was a radical idea at the time; after all, the electromagnetic field had only been discovered in 1865. But Berger found proof. He invented a device called the electroencephalogram (you probably know it as an EEG) that recorded brain waves. Using his new EEG, Berger was the first to demonstrate that our neurons actually talk to one another, and they do so with electrical pulses. He published his results in 1929.

As often happens with revolutionary ideas, Berger's EEG results were either ignored or lambasted as trickery. This was, after all, preternatural activity. But over the course of the next decade, enough independent scholars verified the results that they became widely accepted. Berger saw his findings as evidence of the mind's potential for psychic activity, and he continued searching for more evidence until the day he hanged himself in frustration. The rest of the scientific community went back to what it had always been doing, "good science," and largely forgot about the electric neuron.

That was the case until biophysicist Dr. Eberhard Fetz came along in 1969 and wondered whether what Berger had found could be used more broadly. Dr. Fetz, in an extrapolation of Berger's discovery, reasoned that if brains were controlled by electricity, then perhaps we could use our brains to control electrical devices. Granted, this line of thinking was closer to psychics than physics, but Dr. Fetz proceeded anyway.

In a small primate lab at the University of Washington in Seattle, Fetz connected the brain of a rhesus monkey to an electrical meter and then watched in amazement as the monkey learned how to control the level of the meter. Here was something truly astounding: animals controlling devices with nothing but their thoughts.

While incredible, this insight didn't have much application in 1969. But with the advent of silicon chips, computers, and the internet, the possibilities became unbounded. Imagine what could happen if we traded the meter for a computer chip, the monkey for a person, and enabled humans to connect their brains to the internet. This technology now exists.

A new breed of intelligence is rapidly emerging. The next set of innovations on the horizon will not just come from the brain; it will be part of the brain. Scientists in labs across the globe are busy perfecting computer chips that can be implanted into the human brain. In many ways, the results, if successful, fit squarely in the realm of psychics. There may be no such thing as paranormal activity, but make no mistake that all of the following are possible and on the horizon: telepathy, no problem; telekinesis, absolutely; clairvoyance, without question; ESP, oh yeah.

III

Jan Scheuermann lifted a chocolate bar to her mouth and took a bite. Still chewing, a grin spread across her face as she declared, "one small nibble for a woman, one giant bite for BCI."

BCI stands for brain-computer interface, and Jan is one of only a few people on earth using this technology, through two implanted chips attached directly to the neurons in her brain. The first human brain implant was conceived of by Brown University neuroscientist John Donoghue and implanted into a paralyzed man in 2004. These dime-sized computer chips come from a technology called BrainGate. The BrainGate chip is implanted into the brain and attached to connectors outside of the skull, which are connected to computers that, in Jan Scheuermann's case, were connected to a robotic arm. As a result, Scheuermann can feed herself chocolate by controlling a robotic arm with nothing but her thoughts.

A smart, vibrant woman in her early fifties, Scheuermann has been unable to use her arms and legs since she was diagnosed with a rare genetic disease at the age of 40. "I have not moved things for about ten years . . . This is the ride of my life," she said. "This is the rollercoaster. This is skydiving. It's just fabulous, and I'm enjoying every second of it."

The importance of this research is certainly not lost on Dr. Geoffrey Ling, retired army colonel, neurologist, and manager of the US government agency collaborating on this project. He became interested in brain-controlled prosthetics after seeing countless soldiers lose limbs in Iraq and Afghanistan. "I'm old enough to have watched Neil Armstrong take that step on the moon, and to watch Jan, I had the same tingles, because I realized that we have now stepped over a great threshold into what is possible."

Indeed, this revolutionary technology is world-changing. BrainGate was first featured on *60 Minutes* in 2008, where they showed a paralyzed woman connecting to the internet with her mind. Host Scott Pelley had this to say when introducing the segment: "Once in a while, we run across a science story that is hard to believe until you see it. That's how we felt about this story when we first saw human beings operating computers, writing emails, and driving wheelchairs with nothing but their thoughts." A second piece, featuring Jan Scheuermann, aired in December 2012, and this time Pelley went even further: "We don't use that word [breakthrough] very often because it's overused. But when you see how they've connected this robotic limb to a human brain, you will understand why we made the exception."

Brain-controlled implants have catapulted the threshold of "what is possible" into a whole new dimension. The idea of controlling a device with only the mind sounds like science fiction to many, but it's now an indisputable part of reality. Science, yes; fiction, no. It is no surprise that *60 Minutes* finds it "hard to believe" because it's about as close as science has come to psychic ability. Patients with these implants use their thoughts to communicate, move robotic arms, click icons on a computer screen, and connect to the internet. In the end, Hans Berger was right.

While the BrainGate technology is certainly sophisticated, it's actually quite simple to understand. BrainGate is merely tapping into the brain's electrical signals in the same way that Berger's EEG and Fetz's electrical meter did. The BrainGate chip, once attached to the motor cortex, reads the brain's electrical signals and sends them to a computer, which interprets and sends along instructions to other electrical devices like a robotic arm or a wheelchair. In that respect, it's not much different from using your television remote to change the channel.

The primary goal of doctors and scientists working on this technology is to provide mobility and improved functionality for those with severe disabilities. The potential implications of this research for the disabled cannot be understated. It will enable bionics, restore communication abilities, and give disabled people previously unimaginable access to the world.

While assisting the disabled is the motivation behind Brain-Gate, the implications for the rest of us are equally astounding. Just imagine the ways in which the world will change when we can connect our minds to computers.

IV

Computers have been creeping closer to our brains since their creation. What started as large mainframes became desktops, then laptops, and now tablets and smartphones that we hold only inches from our faces. Google is betting that the next step will be glasses. Its Google Glass project aims to put the internet right in front of your eyes using an interface that is worn like eyeglasses. The device listens to your voice instructions and projects the contents of the internet or any other information you'd like into your perception.

Back in 2004, Google's founders told *Playboy* magazine that one day we'd have direct access to the internet through brain implants, with "the entirety of the world's information as just one of our thoughts." Less than a decade later, the roadmap has been laid. From one side come brain interfaces and from the other comes a faster, more efficient, more personalized internet.

The electrodes implanted in Jan Scheuermann and the small handful of other patients are still the exception rather than the rule. BrainGate, of course, requires brain surgery, which is a serious endeavor. It will take years before an implant is safe enough to be commonplace. But there are a host of brainwave sensors in development for use outside of the skull that will be transformational for all of us.

EdanSafe has developed a product called SmartCap, designed with long-haul trucker safety in mind. A SmartCap is a hat with brain sensors that measure the alertness of drivers. When a driver becomes too fatigued, an alarm is sounded. Clearly, this product has the potential to save lives. Another company, NeuroSky, is working with several major car manufacturers to implant fatigue sensors in car headrests for the non-truckers among us. Your next car could very well include this technology.

Zeo has a wearable EEG headband that measures brain waves. Its first product is an alarm clock that wakes you up in the earliest stage of sleep so that you don't feel groggy in the morning. The *Boston Globe* described it this way: "Rather than waking you up at a precise time—say, 6:30 A.M.—the headband would monitor your brain waves using special sensors, and wake you up sometime in the half-hour leading up to 6:30 when you were in a light phase of sleep, which is preferable to being jolted out of deep sleep." But it is more than that. Zeo also acts as an online sleep coach. It records data, provides you with a sleep score, and compares your sleep patterns to those of others. The *New York Times* noted that this may be the most significant part of Zeo's new technology: "it's truly amazing, if not a little creepy, to see all of this data about a part of your existence that you've known nothing about until now."

The problems of drivers falling asleep and tired sleepers not being able to wake up are far from frivolous. Drowsy driving kills thousands every year, and Zeo's sleep manager is coveted by the millions of Americans with sleep disorders. But brain-sensing technology is being used for fun as well. A company called Emotiv, with its tagline "you think, therefore, you can," has a wearable helmet that measures brain waves to interface with online games. Imagine playing a video game with nothing but your thoughts. The excitement of these products is not lost on the company, which posits "for the first time, the fantasy of magic and supernatural power can be experienced."

Not to be outdone, a company called InteraXon ran an Indiegogo crowdfunding campaign in late 2012, raising a couple hundred thousand dollars to develop its newest product. Among other things, InteraXon has created a beer tap that you turn on and off with your thoughts, and they'll let you use it at your next keg party for a mere $8,500 donation. InteraXon says that its technology will one day allow your mind to control anything with an on/off switch.

Soon you may see people walking around wearing furry cat ears, even when it's not Halloween. These cat ears feature a sensor that presses against the forehead and another that attaches to the ear lobe. Necomimi, the manufacturer, says that the device reads your brain waves to determine your current state of attention or relaxation. When you're highly interested, the ears perk straight up. If you're about to fall asleep, they droop downward. Clearly this isn't serious business—Necomimi calls this product "a fun, quirky addition to parties"—but the science behind it is real. These devices aren't exactly intelligent, but they are pretty smart.

You may say these technologies are frivolous, and you would be mostly right. But a whole new industry is developing around wearable sensors, or neurowear as it's called. The "frivolous" innovations that come from these industries will one day be critical to the least frivolous aspects of our lives. Innovations often spring up in unusual places. Take Tesla, for example. When founder and CEO Elon Musk started the company, his ultimate goal was to mass-produce an electric car, but he couldn't afford it. So he started with a novelty car—an expensive sports car called the Tesla Roadster—in order to supplement the development cost of mass production. "At Tesla, we did, I think, receive some unfair criticism because we had the Tesla Roadster, and people would say, 'Well, why are you making this expensive sports car?' As though we somehow felt that there was a shortage of sports cars for rich people or something. But, in fact, even though I would try to take pains to say, look, our goal from the beginning has been to drive forward the electric car revolution, and we needed time to refine the technology . . . that's where it becomes mass market." Even the very first automobiles were thought of as novelties; much of the world missed the potential impact until after the opportunity to be a first mover had passed.

The same is true for neurowear. Imagine what happens once the bunny ears are perfected and we move on to opening doors or turning on lights. Or instead of operating a beer tap with our thoughts, we start up the fireplace or preheat the oven. Imagine the potential of all the neurogames that are being developed: the underlying technology will one day be used for neurofeedback. This will help untold individuals: it could help those with attention deficits to focus, enable drivers to stay more alert, or aid students in concentration. This is a common cycle of business innovation: businesses leverage in-demand products, no matter how frivolous, to fund new technologies. As a result, technology evolves.

V

Since ancient times, people have been imagining machines that could think. Plato's works included statues that could move and think. Homer's *Iliad* included a god who was accompanied by two golden statues "resembling in all worth, living young damsels, fill'd with minds and wisdom." Even the Hebrew Talmud talks of Golem, a person constructed of clay that could be made to think. The new world has seen through the eyes of HAL, iRobot, and the countless robotic heroes and villains from *Star Wars* and *Star Trek*. We have been attacked by Terminators and loved by Johnny5. We have long had a fascination with—and fear of—what many view as inevitable: that our technological pursuits will one day lead us to thinking machines.

The age of robotics is already upon us. Robots are now being used in virtually every industry. In manufacturing, robots such as the ARC Mate are on the assembly line; in offices, the HRP-4 is delivering mail and getting coffee; in the home, Roomba is doing the cleaning. Two hundred years ago, 70 percent of people were farmers. Now, all but 1 percent of those jobs have been replaced by machines. *Wired Magazine* estimates that in another 100 years, 70 percent of today's occupations will share that same fate.

Robots are interesting, but they haven't quite achieved the goal of artificial intelligence. We have outsourced many physical tasks and even a few mental ones, but creating something in our image has largely eluded us. Computers have always been potential candidates. Even back in 1987, biologist Richard Dawkins went so far as to call computers "honorary living things" in his book *The Blind Watchmaker*. Computers at the time lacked the ability to act as a network of selfless cells, but that has largely changed with the internet.

We are not merely talking about creating a listless biological system; we are talking about intelligence. If we create a life online that rivals the humble sea slug, no one will care. But if we can create something more than the composite of its parts, something that drives us toward greater intelligence—that can reproduce, learn, and drive evolution forward in a way that Darwin couldn't have imagined—then we will have created real intelligence.

Scientists have been racing to build the first intelligent machine, but the pursuit of artificial intelligence has been plagued by problems. The term itself may be the biggest reason: as we create machine intelligence, there will be nothing artificial about it. The field of artificial intelligence, born in the 1950s, began by trying to leverage the strength of computers to overpower human intelligence. The thought was that, with enough speed and brute force, computers could do anything that brains could do. After all, an average laptop computer can calculate five million times faster than the human mind. This approach had some success creating artificial intelligence. But it was artificial. Gammonoid quickly became the world's best backgammon player in the 1970s. In the 1990s, the computer Deep Blue crushed its human competition at the game of chess. In 2011, IBM's Watson computer became the Jeopardy world champion. But all of these computers were horribly bad sports: they couldn't say hello, shake hands, or make small talk of any kind. These are big brooding machines with immense storage and calculating power but not much more. Artificial intelligence has proved woefully inept at creating real intelligence.

The newest trend is to reverse engineer the brain. As the theory goes, once we understand all of the brain's parts, we can re-create them to build an intelligent system. But there are two problems with this approach. First, we don't actually understand the brain currently. The brain, especially in terms of its parts, is largely still a mystery. Neuroscience is making tremendous progress, but it is still early. New research constantly overwrites prior theory. That is a problem with science in general: science does not deal in facts, only theories. Scientists labor to prove things wrong, but they can never actually prove something right. Eventually, we can have a large degree of confidence, but perfect knowledge just doesn't exist. The newer the field, the greater the likelihood that current theories will be undermined by future research.

Even something as simple as the number of neurons in our brains is hotly debated. In the 1970s and again in late 2000, the prevailing theory was that we had only around 86 billion neurons; today, convention pegs it at 100 billion, roughly the same number as what we thought through the 1980s and 1990s. New research is again contesting that number. Neuroscientists' estimates have been as low as 10 billion and as high as 1 trillion. And that's not even considering the controversy surrounding our (supposed) 100 trillion neural connections or the trillions of surrounding glial cells.

The second issue with reverse engineering the brain is more fundamental. Just as the Wright brothers didn't learn to fly by dissecting birds, we will not learn to create intelligence by re-creating a brain. The Wright Flyer looked nothing like a bird, but it flew just the same. We can use the brain as a rough guide just as the Wrights used birds as a guide, but ultimately intelligence will emerge in its own way.

To be sure, there is plenty to learn from biology. The Wrights took what concepts they could from the flight of birds and applied them: wingspans, velocity, aerodynamics. But they left most of the rest—the feathers, beak, and organs—for the birds. Gaining an understanding of something biological doesn't mean you will be able to build or engineer it.

The internet has a real shot at intelligence, but it is pretty clear that it will look nothing like a 3-pound wrinkly lump of clay, nor will it have cells or blood or fat. Those are all critical to brains but not to intelligence. In that way, we may never create an artificial brain, but the intelligence will be very much real. Dan Dennett, who was an advocate of reverse engineering at one point, put it this way: "I'm trying to undo a mistake I made some years ago, and rethink the idea that the way to understand the mind is to take it apart."

Dennett's mistake was to reduce the brain to the neuron in an attempt to rebuild it. But that is reducing the brain one step too far, pushing us from the edge of the forest to deep into the trees. This is the danger in any kind of reverse engineering. Biologists reduced colonies down to ants, but we have now learned that the ant network, the colony, is the critical level. Reducing flight to the feathers of a bird would not have worked, but reducing it to the wingspan did the trick. Feathers are one step too far, just as are ants and neurons.

Unfortunately, scientists have oversimplified the function of a neuron, treating it merely as a predictable switching device that fires on and off. That would be incredibly convenient if it were true. But neurons are only logical when they work; they are more fallible than they are predictable. Remember, a neuron misfires up to 90 percent of the time. Artificial intelligence almost universally ignores this fact. One can't possibly build artificial intelligence by looking at a single, highly faulty neuron. So rather than focus on something else, the field just assumes that neurons are predictable.

Focusing on a single neuron's on/off switch misses what is fundamentally happening with the *network* of neurons. The neuron is faulty but the network performs amazing feats. The faultiness of the individual neuron allows for the plasticity and adaptive nature of the network as a whole. Intelligence cannot be replicated by creating a bunch of switches, faulty or not. Instead, we must focus on the network.

Neurons may be good analogs for transistors and maybe even computer chips, but they're not good building blocks of intelligence. The neural network is fundamental. The BrainGate technology works because the chip attaches not to a single neuron, but to a network of neurons. Reading the signals of a single neuron would tell us very little; it certainly wouldn't allow BrainGate patients to move a robotic arm or a computer cursor. Scientists may never be able to reverse engineer the neuron, but they are increasingly able to interpret the communication of the network.

It is for this reason that the internet is a better candidate for intelligence than are computers. Computers are perfect calculators composed of perfect transistors; they are like the neurons we once thought we had in our brains. But the internet has all the quirkiness of the brain: it can work in parallel, it can communicate across broad distances, and it makes mistakes. The internet is at an early stage in its evolution, but it can leverage the brain that nature has given us. It took millions of years for humans to gain intelligence, but it may only take a century for the internet. The convergence of computer networks and neural networks is the key to creating real intelligence from artificial machines.

VI

In the 1950s, Princeton University mathematical physics professor John von Neumann coined the term "singularity" to refer to the time when machines gain human intelligence. It is a fascinating concept, the point at which we achieve real artificial intelligence. The idea of a singularity has been thoroughly examined by famed MIT inventor Ray Kurzweil, author of *The Singularity Is Near,* who has said he believes it will happen in 2045.

But singularities don't happen in nature. Evolution is a slow, laborious process. Our intelligence evolved over millions of years. Oftentimes we don't even notice evolution when it happens: it took us 20,000 years to realize that our brains were shrinking. If a singularity exists, it is naive to think that we will recognize when it happens. We will not pass through some event horizon that changes history overnight and gives us intelligent machines. It has been evolving and will continue to evolve with the insights of our scientists—the Donoghues and Dennetts—and our innovators—the Fetzes and Bergers. Von Neumann was well aware of this; he even noted that the singularity of which he spoke was really just a sign that something was on the horizon.

To some extent, we've already reached a singularity. Robots, computers, and the internet all show intelligence. And with Brain-Gate, we have fused mind and machine: neurons providing intelligence to computers. Who needs computers that think when we can have people who think with computers? In that respect, we have already made it through the von Neumann singularity.

In another way, however, we will never reach a singularity. In our quest to create intelligent machines, we keep changing the rules. In the 1960s, we said a computer that could beat a backgammon champion would surely be intelligent. But when Gammonoid beat Luigi Villa, the world champion backgammon player, by a score of 7–1, we decided to rethink our definition. We reasoned in hindsight that backgammon is relatively easy; it's a game of straightforward calculations. We changed the rules to focus on games of sophisticated rules and strategies. Backgammon is easy by that definition, but chess is another story. Yet when IBM's Deep Blue computer beat reigning chess champion Gary Kasparov in 1997, we changed the rules again. No longer were sophisticated calculations or logical decision making acts of intelligence. Perhaps when computers could answer human knowledge questions, then they'd be intelligent. Of course, we had to revise that theory in 2011 when IBM's Watson computer soundly beat the best humans at Jeopardy.

We have done the same thing in nature. It was previously thought that what sets us apart from other animals was our ability to use tools. Then we saw primates and crows using tools. So we changed our minds and said that what makes us intelligent is our ability to use language. Then biologists taught the first chimpanzee how to use sign language, and we decided that intelligence couldn't be about language after all. Next came self-consciousness and awareness until experiments unequivocally proved that dolphins are self-aware.

With animal intelligence as well as artificial intelligence, we keep changing the goalposts. We draw a line in the sand, we reach that line, and then we cross it out and draw a new line further down. Events leading toward artificial intelligence have been happening for hundreds of years, but there is no one big event that will happen to generate the headline "the singularity is here." We have already reached a singularity and will never reach a singularity. The inevitable conclusion may elude us, but it is no less a fact: artificial intelligence is real, it's here, and it will continue to evolve.

ELEVEN

CONCLUSION | TERMITES | EXTINCTION

I n 1994, five biologists found three large, fully mature leaf-cutter ant nests in Botucatu, Brazil. As any good scientists would do, they set out to explore the nests. They poured over a ton of cement into one of the nests, waited days for it to harden, and then started digging.

When fully excavated, the preserved nests were a sight to behold. A marvel of modern engineering, one mound covered an above-ground surface area of nearly 725 square feet. The largest nest had tunnels extending 229 feet below the earth, making the entire structure as large as a skyscraper and as wide as a city block. Its construction required the ants to move untold tons of soil.

The extensive labyrinths of the largest nest contained 7,863 chambers reaching as far down as 23 feet, each with a specific purpose: there were garden compartments, nurseries, even trash heaps. The tunnel system connecting the chambers looked like a superhighway system, complete with on-ramps, off-ramps, and local access roads. The structure itself looked as if it had been designed by an architect.

Leaf-cutter ants are known to build some of the most elaborate homes across the entire animal kingdom. In many cases, they dig chambers directly into the water table, allowing for a natural source of hydration. At the surface of leaf-cutter mounds are hundreds of openings, allowing for ventilation. Openings in the center of the mound blow out hot air and carbon dioxide from within the nest, creating an inflow of outside air from the holes at the periphery of the nest mound. In this way, cool fresh air continuously circulates throughout the nest. The ants use principles of wind velocity and thermal convection to regulate gas exchange, and this advanced air-conditioning system is important for more than just ant comfort.

Many people have witnessed ants carrying large objects, and those who live in Central America, South America, and the southern United States often see ants carrying leaves. They look as if they're holding up tiny leaf-umbrellas, so much so that Texas and Louisiana residents call them "parasol ants." Most people would be surprised to learn that leaf-cutter ants don't actually eat the leaves they diligently cut down and haul back to the nest.

Instead, leaf-cutter ants eat fungus that they nurture, fertilize, and harvest themselves. The fungus thrives on leaves, hence all the leaf cutting and transporting. The fungus also requires precise temperatures and humidity levels, and the ants regulate those levels by plugging up holes used for inflow and outflow, depending on whether the fungus needs more humidity or more cool air. If drastic changes are required, the ants will even transport the whole fungus crop to more hospitable chambers within the nest.

Of course, as we have seen with other ant endeavors, leaf-cutter colonies differ in their proficiency levels. Smaller, younger colonies close up their nest entrances during rain to prevent flooding, which leads to high carbon dioxide levels and suboptimal fungus growth conditions. Larger, mature colonies—those who are past the stage of breakpoint—work around this problem. Their numerous nest openings and deeper chambers enable the ants to allow carbon dioxide gases to escape while maintaining a low risk of flooding.

Mature African termite colonies do something very similar. They build high-rises—mounds averaging six to ten feet tall—and they tend to their fungus gardens within. Like those of the leaf-cutter ants, the termites' fungi are temperamental and can only survive within a narrow temperature range. But the outside temperatures vary drastically in some parts of Africa, sometimes dropping to 35 degrees Fahrenheit at night and heating to 104 degrees during the day. To compensate, the termites spend their days opening and closing existing vents, digging new vents, and plugging up old ones.

Like ants, termites aren't smart; an individual termite could not possibly have enough neural firepower to conceptualize a termite mound. But the termite colony, just like an ant colony, is something different. Once the termite colony hits its breakpoint, which varies with each of the roughly 2,800 species of termite, the colony gains intelligence.

Luckily for us, the human brain is big enough to replicate the termite mounds. Zimbabwean architect Mick Pearce, long fascinated by termite colonies, designed a replica building in Harare called the Eastgate Centre. The building is the country's largest retail and office space facility, and it uses no traditional air conditioning despite the African heat. Instead, it uses the ventilation systems long employed by termites and leaf-cutter ants. Hot air is drawn out through tall chimneys while cool air is sucked in from the building's large open space, strategically located to collect natural breezes. The building uses a mere 10 percent of the amount of energy consumed by similarly sized buildings in the area. Unsurprisingly, the biomimetic building has been hailed as revolutionary, and Pearce has won numerous awards.

Pearce's accomplishment was astounding, and his accolades are well deserved. But we should be equally impressed by the mimicked as by the mimicker. It's far easier for us to recognize human genius than to acknowledge the smarts of a termite or an ant. Clearly, we are biased. Perhaps it's not that we are terribly species-centric, but that we fail to recognize the impact of networks across the board. This includes all of the various networks of which we're a part: our families, our schools, our cities, and the vast network of *Homo sapiens* on this planet.

Pearce didn't act alone to build the Eastgate Centre, and that's not just because hundreds of designers, engineers, and construction workers were involved. Since birth, Pearce benefited from mankind's collective knowledge and experiences. If Pearce's mother took prenatal vitamins or received other prenatal medical care, he benefited from the human network even in the womb. As a young child, he likely built his first building with toy blocks, perfected over time by toymakers for maximum stimulation and safety. He went to school and learned about mathematics, geology, and physics, subjects that even the wisest professors could not have understood were it not for their predecessors and contemporaries.

None of this knowledge is genetic. Pearce's DNA contains the instructions for lots of things: breathing, eating, vocalizing. Theoretically, Pearce would have done those things even with no guidance from other humans. Our DNA also contains the code that allows us to make calculations, store memories, and learn new things. But even the humans among us with the most genetically endowed brainpower would remain primitive if born on a deserted island, if they even survived at all.

|

We are born into rich, healthy networks, and these networks make us vastly more intelligent, efficient, and capable than our mere biology allows. It is a concept known as "emergence," where complex systems emerge from simple parts. In their book *Connected: The Surprising Power of Our Social Networks and How They Shape Our Lives,* Nicholas Christakis and James Fowler explain it this way: "The idea of emergence can be understood with an analogy: A cake has a taste not found in any one of its ingredients. Nor is its taste simply the average of the ingredients' flavors—something, say, halfway between flour and eggs. It is much more than that. The taste of cake transcends the simple sum of its ingredients. Likewise, understanding social networks allows us to understand how indeed, in the case of humans, the whole comes to be greater than the sum of its parts."

In his famous essay "I, Pencil," Nobel Prize–winning economist Leonard Read points out just how complex even the most simple emergent systems have become. Read demonstrates how something as simple as a pencil is astonishingly hard for one person to make. Humans create billions of them per year, but no single individual knows how to do it on his own. A few people know how to combine the rapeseed oil from the Dutch East Indies with the sulfur chloride and the cadmium sulfide in just the right combination to make the little pink eraser. Others know how to turn petroleum into the paraffin needed for the smooth lacquer coat. Still others know how to make the string that ties together the paper sacks in which the graphite is packed for shipping after it is mined in Sri Lanka. The list goes on ad nauseam. It takes a huge network to create something as simple as a pencil. As scientist Matt Ridley points out, "we've created the ability to do things that we don't even understand . . . We've gone beyond the capacity of the human mind to an extraordinary degree." We expanded our minds, not with technology, but with networks.

This is true of all highly social species. The secret of the ant's evolutionary success, like ours, is networks. Ants are tremendously diverse, but what they have in common, as biologist Bert Hölldobler explains, is that "they all live in societies; they all are social insects. There is not a single ant species known that lives solitarily. The evolutionary transition from a solitary life to a social life occurred only in about 3 to 5% of all animal species, including our own species, Homo sapiens. But this minority plays an overwhelmingly dominant role in almost all land habitats." Like those of humans, the social networks of ants enable them to have emergent properties and dominate the landscape.

Through communication and cooperation, ants are able to do things that no other animals can do, even much smarter, bigger-brained animals. In May 2012, *Discovery News* ran the headline "Human Societies Starting to Resemble Ant Colonies." This article outlined Smithsonian researcher Mark Moffett's perspective that while our DNA is most similar to that of chimpanzees, "no chimpanzee group has to deal with issues of public health, infrastructure, distribution of goods and services, market economies, mass transit problems, assembly lines and complex teamwork, agriculture and animal domestication, warfare and slavery." He added that "ants have developed behaviors addressing all of these problems."

II

The world is a dangerous place. Of all the species that have ever existed on earth, 99.9 percent have gone extinct. But the success rate seems to be better for the most networked animals. Most of nature's known social animals still exist—ants, termites, bees, wasps, and us. Even so, survival is tough. More than 90 percent of harvester ant colonies fail in their first year. (Though if they reach the breakpoint, most of the remaining 10 percent will survive another 20 to 25 years on average, sending many reproductive queens out into the world.)

Not only are networks vital to our success, they're vital to our intelligence. Post-breakpoint, networks are much, much more intelligent than any individual member of the network. It's true for humans as much as for any other species, and it's similarly true for technological networks. After all, our technology networks—the internet, the web, Facebook—are just tools to further connect our human network.

The important point is this: social networks after the breakpoint are highly successful both in the short term (the life of the network) and the long term (the survival of the species). This extends to the individuals that make up the network as well: a social animal living outside the network won't last long. Imagine a baby ant, or even a baby human, somehow forced to live without the support of others. Neither is likely to survive. Social animals do not fare well outside of their networks. On the other hand, an infant grasshopper, snake, or even a kitten stands a much better chance.

Social animals also do not fair well when their networks grow too large. UCLA scientist Jared Diamond argues that we became disconnected from our social networks as a result of the population boom during the agricultural revolution, which he calls "the worst mistake in the history of the human race." We parted ways with the egalitarian, antlike hunter-gatherer societies in which we had survived and thrived for hundreds of thousands of years. Of course, agriculture allowed our populations to explode (perhaps causing us to overshoot our carrying capacity, the subject of Diamond's book *Collapse*). Agriculture enabled large-scale food production in which a few farmers could feed many people, allowing cities to be built. Subsequently, people came in contact with many more people than previously—hunter-gatherer tribes rarely grew beyond 150 members or so. We fundamentally changed the structure of our networks from democratic, antlike "colonies," so to speak, to a more complex hierarchical system.

The printing press, the industrial revolution, and the digital revolution made the human network more efficient and intelligent. The network revolution is changing us even more drastically. Of course, we are both collectively and individually smarter as a result of our unprecedented access to the world's information—and thanks to improved search capabilities, we can access that information at unprecedented speed. But the changes brought about by the internet are even more fundamental than that.

The internet both connects us more deeply and levels the playing field between us. For example, ten years ago, it was easier for a dictator to survive with massive disconnects between what he promised and what he delivered; there was no real vehicle to tease that apart en masse. Now there is a vehicle, and in recent years we've seen analysts credit social media networks with helping Middle Eastern protesters organize demonstrations, share information, and report to the rest of the world. The web in general and social media in particular, by their very nature, promote democracy and present challenges for dictators attempting to pass off as fact anything other than the truth. Even the dictators know this. In January 2011, the Egyptian government instructed all of the country's internet service providers to pull the plug. With only four ISPs, all of which were obligated to obey government orders, it was relatively easy for Egypt to cut off its citizens from the outside world.

Of course, this wouldn't be possible in the United States or Europe as there are hundreds of ISPs with distributed redundancy throughout the internet. As the internet grows in the Middle East, it will become increasingly difficult to do such a thing there as well. Our human network is getting both deeper and broader, and the network itself is more powerful than any dictator. In a sense, the democratization of the web is reversing the hierarchies brought about by agriculture and returning us to the tight-knit networks that have allowed humans to thrive throughout history.

III

Of course, networks must get through a breakpoint and reach equilibrium before they are of real value to us. Just as our brains aren't wise until they hit a breakpoint and prune neurons and connections, the networks that connect our brains to those of others must be allowed to mature. For technology networks, this means encouraging growth at all costs and avoiding monetization too early; but it also means shifting gears once the breakpoint is reached.

The results of patience are well worth it, both for corporations that must satisfy stakeholders and for humanity as a whole. The result of mature, fully functioning networks is a more tightly knit world with capabilities well beyond the sum of our abilities.

The network revolution has changed the game permanently, and this is just the beginning. What is to come will be more exciting than ever. Technology is on the verge of creating the types of things habitually reserved for humans: consciousness, intelligence, and emotion. The future will be limited only by the limits of the greatest imaginations of our technological and biological networks.

TWELVE

AFTERWORD:
THE INTERNET IS A BRAIN

Throughout this book, the internet has been used as an analog to the brain because both are complex networks. But there are even more fundamental similarities, which I would argue are evidence that the internet is not merely *like* a brain but *is* a brain. While not central to the concept of breakpoint, these ideas are significant in developing a full understanding of the potential of the internet, especially as it relates to artificial intelligence.

The important question is this: Could the internet itself be made to perform more like a brain or even perform the functions of a brain—just as a hearing aid performs the function of the inner ear, or a contact lens performs the function of the cornea, or an artificial heart performs the function of that biological muscle?

A computer is generally a poor analogy to a brain. It's true that semiconductors switch on and off like neurons, and that fibers of glass can transmit messages like synapses and axons, but that's where the analogy ends. Our computers are not nearly as analogous to the brain as, for example, an artificial heart is to a real heart.

The internet, however, is unlike anything humankind has built before. All of our previous inventions—steam locomotives, television sets, cars—are inert. Chessboards and baseball stadiums may flicker to life momentarily, but go dark when the game is done. The internet is different. It's unbounded, self-perpetuating, and capable of collective consciousness. It's more like the crowd watching the baseball game than the stadium itself.

Of course, every innovation that delivers something greater than the sum of its parts is miraculous. Alexander Graham Bell attached two small drums to two wire coils and out of those bits created something beyond the sum of the parts: sound. But the telephone did not go on to replicate and improve itself. The internet can and does. And beyond that, the internet learns. It processes information, shapes it, transmits it. It remembers some things, forgets others, and constantly loops whatever it has again and again, spinning it in as many ways and in as many directions as one could imagine.

I

Without a strong understanding of what a brain actually is, it may seem preposterous to say that the internet is a brain. The internet is not the three-pound wrinkled gray glob that most of us conjure up as an image of the brain. Actually, that's not even what the brain is. The brain is nearly 60 percent white matter—the tissue that connects neurons—with only the remainder being the gray stuff we typically think of. The gray matter contains the all-important neurons, but the connections are equally important.

Outside of the deep ridges and two hemispheres, most people wouldn't recognize a brain if presented with one. The brain is very soft, almost jellylike, and ivory in color with deep burgundy-colored veins. The brain doesn't take on a firm gray appearance until it's dead, bloodless, and preserved. This visual distinction is important because it tells us that a living brain is consuming massive amounts of energy in the form of blood flow.

But even that description is somewhat misleading. In the way the brain actually functions, it is far more similar to a piece of paper. The paper represents the outermost area of the brain, the cerebral cortex. It is here that most of the magic of thought takes place. Imagine this piece of paper: thin, rectangular, and mostly blank to start. On the paper are bits of information that grow as the brain is formed, like braille embossed on the page. Those are the neurons, and they help to store and process information.

The ingenuity of the brain comes not from the informational elements but from how that information is physically connected. Imagine crumpling the piece of paper into a ball. Two dots at either end of the page are far away from each other initially. But as you crumple the paper, the dots get closer. Crumple it enough times, and every point will be in striking distance of every other point. Our brains are folded and crumpled into our skulls in just this manner, and their unique power comes from the ability to connect disparate pieces of information for quick communication and interdisciplinary learning.

In terms of the computer industry, the human brain is a sophisticated "parallel processing" machine. That means that it does a number of things at the same time, unlike "serial computing" in which one thing happens, then another, and then another. Neuroscientists call this "distributed computing," meaning that since the functions of the brain are distributed all over the place, things can happen simultaneously. ("Distributed" is a more accurate term than "parallel" because parallel computing conjures up the idea of two unbending parallel lines, like railroad tracks, whereas "distributed" is a freewheeling image that describes more accurately how the brain actually works.)

A neuron consists of the soma, an axon, and dendrites. Think of the soma as the center of the neuron or the information clearinghouse. The axon acts as a transmitter, sending information from one neuron to another. The dendrites receive information from other neurons. Neurons communicate with one another through electrical and chemical transmitters. These tightly packed neurons work together in a distributed network, forming patterns that allow us to perform tasks such as walking, speaking, remembering someone's name, and even reading this book.

II

The fact that the brain is an ordinary organ is actually a good thing in terms of trying to create an artificial mind. It frees us to speculate that an intelligent internet is possible. We've always considered the brain to be a sacred organ in a sacred chalice, but to many philosophers, scientists, and more than a few internet entrepreneurs, the idea of mechanized thinking is no longer beyond the question, "Why not?"

Never before has the idea of a "thinking machine" brought together a greater confluence of thinkers and scientists. They range from neurologists, who are dissecting the brain with greater skill and instruments; to psychologists, who are understanding behavior that emerges from the brain; to linguists, who recognize how thoughts are put into the symbols that we call words; to evolutionary scientists, who are developing a new field called genetic engineering; to computer scientists, who are building machines and algorithms that mimic the mind; and to artificial intelligence types, who are focusing intently on getting machines to actually think.

Of course, even among this group of distinguished thinkers, there is no consensus on how to create artificial intelligence. Tufts

University philosopher Dan Dennett notes in his book *Consciousness Explained,* "No one can keep all the problems clear, including me, and everyone has to mumble, guess, and hand wave about
large parts of the problem." The voices are many, the opinions
sharply different, but in this burgeoning world of brain science
and technology, we are finally seeing a convergence on the idea
that a thinking machine is inevitable. And, consequently, that this
newfound intelligence will affect our lives profoundly.

What is bringing this diverse group of people together is the
internet. The reason, of course, is that the internet is very similar
in structure to the brain, in that it's mainly a massive storage,
calculation, and communication system. The internet is clunkier
and smaller than the brain (neurons versus computers, not sheer
size or weight), but the fundamental structure is roughly the same.
The brain has neurons and memories while the internet has computers and websites, connected together through cables and hy-
perlinks instead of axons and dendrites.

Of course, something may look like something else and not
have a connection. The switching system of a phone network looks
something like a neural network, but it isn't. Yet there are things
about the internet that make this similarity too strong to resist.

Remember, the internet is really the combination of two innovations. The first was the telephone, which allowed information to be
transmitted electronically. With the advent of the telephone, people
could communicate instantaneously across enormous distances and
through the most difficult terrain. This seems obvious to us now,
but it was unimaginable during the days of the Pony Express.

The second innovation was the computer, which allowed us to
process and store large amounts of information. Before the computer, we processed information using calculating devices and
then wrote down the results on paper. Complex calculations, the

type even the most modest laptop does without breaking a sweat, were virtually impossible before the computer. And if we needed to store valuable or large amounts of information, like a book manuscript, for example, the best options were to put it either under a mattress or in a bank.

Both the telephone and the computer solved huge problems, but combining the two and creating the internet created revolutionary opportunities. The modern-day internet may simply be a set of computers hooked together by telephone lines, but this simple yet powerful amalgamation allows us to store, process, and transmit information.

The internet is uniquely powerful because it has hundreds of millions of computers connected to each other, all sharing information and working on your behalf as you sit in your house searching for "vegan brownie recipes" on Google. Like the neurons in the brain, the internet processes information in parallel across its millions of computers.

The human brain has around 100 billion neurons. In another 20 years or so, the number of computers connected to the internet will arrive at a comparable total. In time, the internet will approximate the complexity of the brain. Think of it this way: it took hundreds of thousands of years for the human brain to evolve to its current level of complexity and sophistication. The internet will approximate that in a few generations. We will have experienced in cyberspace a replication of biological growth itself, as though it were a living brain. But more specifically, we will not merely replicate the brain itself, we will duplicate the brain's byproduct: thought.

III

We can't create intelligence until we know the answer to a fundamental question: What characterizes human thought? "A period of mulling," said the late University of Chicago professor How-ard Margolis, "followed by periods of recapitulation, in which we describe to ourselves what seems to have gone on during the mulling." In other words, the human mind thinks in a series of loop-de-loops. The brain is wired to be parallel, which allows our thoughts to be recursive.

As a result, the human brain is a lousy computing machine. To behave like the human brain, a computer would have to do this: Start searching for an item with fierce concentration, then back off a little, then jump back in, then find itself staring blankly out the window, then off to a warm reverie—shafts of sunlight bouncing off the green grass or something like that—then sud-denly, bang, back to reality with an abrupt epiphany: "Got to put Puppy Chow on the grocery list." That's how humans think. Even logical thinking, the kind you might expect from a rocket scientist or a McKinsey strategist, is more like a playful dolphin doing loop-de-loops and acrobatic tumbles than a shark torpedo-ing toward prey. We can't help it. That's the way the brain works.

Pulitzer Prize–winning brain scientist Douglas Hofstadter de-scribes the process in his book *I Am a Strange Loop*. He argues that consciousness is an endless loop, where the brain takes the information it's fed from the environment and other brains and constantly edits it in an elusive and self-repeating manner. In other words, thoughts travel from brain to mouth to ear to brain, round and round, until internal consciousness arises.

Not coincidentally, this is also how we learn. "We human be-ings have used our plasticity not only to learn, but to learn how to learn better," Dennett says. We repeat and repeat and repeat something until it becomes better and better and better. This is the primary thesis behind Malcolm Gladwell's bestseller *Outliers*, in which he argues that the greatest achievements of humankind have come not from genius but from reiterative practice.

For an artificial brain to be similar to a human brain, it must have the same loopy and iterative processes. Humanlike thinking will not come from more powerful computers or from building on the strengths of artificial intelligence but from a network approach that mimics the weaknesses of human thinking. In other words, we need to create a machine that stops calculating from time to time to gaze out the window. We don't need supercomputers to do that.

If we can create a machine that guesses, fumbles, rounds off, and is not very good with numbers, we will be closer to replicating the human mind. We will also need the machine to be recursive: it should continuously edit itself, make little changes, test out potential answers against problems, and discard losing ideas. Most importantly, we need a machine that learns through repetition, and that would prefer to be half-right than completely right. In other words, we need a prediction machine.

IV

The brain is a slow, inefficient machine. Transmissions to the cerebral cortex range from one to thirty meters per second along the axons and about one-third of a meter per second along dendrites. In comparison, light travels at about 300 million meters per second. So the brain is quite sluggish compared to the transmission speed of a computer or a fiber optic network. Moreover, it takes a neuron two thousandths of a second to snap on and off in your head. A computer does the same thing a million times faster. Neurons fire on average at about one hundred times per second (technically they can get up to several hundred pulses per second, but then they retreat in exhaustion). This pales in comparison to the transistor in your smartphone.

Given the brain's slow processing speed, humans must try to keep *predicting* what will happen. For its part, the brain helps us to guess better by rewarding our correct guesses. The rewards are little spurts of dopamine (the same substance that is overproduced when an addict uses a drug like heroin) that are distributed throughout the brain's 500,000 dopamine neurons. This reward process coaxes out smart thinking.

Suppose you have a piece of chocolate in front of you. Your brain predicts that it is going to taste good, based on past experience, and your hand reaches for it and drops it into your mouth. Over time, the brain makes other associations and connections so that, eventually, even the word Godiva yields a similar biological reaction.

The results are similar for emotionally laden concepts such as freedom of speech, higher taxes, motherhood, or apple pie. For many of these, the brain's reaction is preconfigured based on past experience: the pattern is set beforehand because the brain has already placed a value on the concept. Therefore, the brain doesn't have to do any fresh thinking. It has predicted its reaction.

Humans use anticipation every minute of every day, for both big and small things. When you spin a cup of coffee around so that the handle has moved from the left to the right side, your mind doesn't go about reexamining the entire cup. It doesn't need to start from scratch. It knows from previous experience that the mug of coffee is the same. It just fills in the change in the handle. Similarly, when we step out the front door in the morning, our brains know what to expect. Memory serves us well; the patterns are there. If you step out your front door in the morning and find a dead body on your sidewalk, you will certainly note that. But you don't examine the oak tree in the front yard as though it had never existed before.

What's really interesting about this is that Plato, in his theory of forms, stated that a perfect tree, a perfect flower, a perfect model of everything exists in the ether of the heavens. For centuries, philosophers have explored the meaning of this. But now, brain science offers some new enlightenment: our brains hold perfect representations of things—memory patterns—that can be efficiently called upon. To that prototypical image, the brain merely makes a quick comparison, noting whatever is new. These memory patterns, of course, enable predictions, preemptive expectations of what we will see. They are, in the words of Steven Pinker, "the internal simulation of possible behaviors and their anticipated consequences."

Making predictions is not just the work of the brain regions that enable reasoning and decision making. Many predictions are driven by the amygdala, an almond-shaped cluster of interconnected structures perched above the brainstem near the bottom of the limbic ring. The amygdala is the seat not of reason but of passion and emotion. It turns out that emotion plays an important role in predictions. In fact, in times of emergency, the amygdala often springs into action before the rationally thinking neocortex has time to make a decision.

Imagine seeing a rattlesnake in your path: the visual signal instantly goes from the retina to the visual cortex, which gets the first pass at the coiled object. Then it passes the information on to the neocortex for analysis and to the hippocampus for storage in memory. All of that is straightforward. But recently, researchers have noted that part of that signal goes in a different direction. Here we have a perfect example of parallel processing in action. The information also goes directly from the visual cortex to the highly emotional amygdala. Since the amygdala can house memories, those memories can make us respond even without "knowing" the reason. We don't wait around to finish analyzing the slithering object on the ground; we jump.

"While the hippocampus remembers the dry facts, the amygdala retains the emotional flavor that goes with those facts—that means that the brain has two memory systems, one for ordinary facts and one for emotionally charged ones," says psychologist and author of the widely acclaimed book *Emotional Intelligence*, Daniel Goleman. "Just as there is a steady murmur of background thoughts in the mind, there is a constant emotional hum." What's particularly interesting is that, unlike other parts of our brains, the amygdala is fully formed at birth. It's so important to our survival that it was given developmental priority.

Our brains are far more distributed than we once thought. We have a brain that sees patterns rather than individual pixels of information; a brain that is anticipating with pre-stored knowledge; a brain that has intuition and insight. And the really good news is that, with time, it only gets better. Sure, the neurons in our brains die, but our wisdom blossoms.

V

The brain can arrive at answers through intuition that no computer, regardless how powerful, could ever conceive of. The internet, in contrast to computers, is already scratching the surface of the brain's insight through intuition. Several companies are building software online that leverages the brain to create what we think of as human consciousness. Brain scientist Doug Lenat has been working on one such intelligent system, called CYC, for the past 20 years. Ask Lenat when he thinks CYC will be conscious, and his response is bold: "I think it's conscious now."

For the internet to be a true brain, it needs to combine calculation, communication, prediction capabilities, and loopiness. When these functions can perform in parallel in the haphazard way of the brain, humanlike intelligence will spread out across the internet. As Google's chairman Erik Schmidt highlighted many years ago, "when the network becomes as fast as the processor, the computer hollows out and spreads across the network."

Some systems on the internet will almost certainly reach the level of consciousness that we reserve only for the smartest of animals, including humans. But despite the optimism of Doug Lenat, we are not there yet. We are close, however. We have perfected calculation and memory to a level greater than human capacity. The internet's ability to communicate is also advanced; in many respects, it is approaching 80 percent of human capacity. The prediction capabilities of the internet have grown stronger over time, although they are still only about 30 percent of what a human mind can do; good but not yet good enough. As scientists and businesses continue to work on these elements, we move closer to the gray area of intelligence, and eventually the internet will have enough gray matter itself to emerge with wisdom and consciousness.

By far the weakest component is the concept of loopiness—the ability for us to combine disparate pieces of information into a coherent pattern. But even there, great strides have been made. The journal *Science* reported in 2012 on a new brain model called Spaun. This neural network can mimic behavior, recognize syntax, and determine patterns by replicating the loopiness of the human brain. Spaun achieves this using only 2.5 million synthetic neurons. While this pales in comparison to the human brain, Spaun can predict the answers to IQ questions such as filling in the pattern of "2, 4, 8, 16, 32, __." Spaun has a 94 percent accuracy rating for image recognition, as compared to a control group of humans who have roughly a 98 percent accuracy rating. It is not 100 percent accurate, and that is the point—Spaun is replicating an imperfect mind.

Spaun's methods are loopy: the scientists did not use standard computer software to teach it how to calculate; instead, they created spiking neurons that mimic the behavior of humans. As the lead researcher, Dr. Chris Eliasmith, remarked, "This model is trying to address that issue of cognitive flexibility. How do we switch between tasks, how do we use the same components in our head to do all those different tasks?" He went on to add that Spaun's mistakes, not its accomplishments, are what is most surprising. The process of finding a solution is quite haphazard for Spaun— it uses endless loops and makes the same errors that the human brain does. It takes in all the available information, discards what it deems irrelevant, meanders a bit, and comes up with an answer that is occasionally foolish, but often correct.

The *New York Times* reported that, "from the billions of documents that form the World Wide Web and the links that weave them together, computer scientists and a growing collection of start-up companies are finding new ways to mine human intelligence." We are living in an epic time, in which machines are growing more intelligent every day. We are approaching the time in which all the information on the internet will be crumpled like our paper model of the brain, where patterns will be established, and where multiple drafts will live and die. The result will be the emergence of intelligence.

ACKNOWLEDGMENTS

Breakpoint grew out of an article I wrote for the *Harvard Business Review*, and much of the thesis has been influenced by the articles I have written since, as well as the feedback I have received from my editors, peer reviewers, and commentators at Harvard. The book could not have been completed without the tremendous help of Lindsey Long. When she started this process, she was my executive assistant, but she has found her calling working on the book, which will inevitably lead to more writing-intensive roles. Lindsey's tireless work improved the book in more ways than I can describe, and she participated in virtually every aspect, including challenging me on many of the underlying theories. I also owe thanks to my editor, Laurie Harting, whose efforts improved the book with each of the many drafts she reviewed. Early versions of the book were also reviewed by a number of individuals who provided constructive feedback: William Allen, Paul Allopenna, Lydia Blalock, Erik Calonius, Peter Delgrosso, Dan Dennett, Reid Fahs, Finn Faldi, John Griffen, Judy Hackett, David Hughes, Alex Kazerani, Caitlin Mason, Sara Mathew, Lars Pettersson, Cheryl Stibel, and John Suh. The graphs and illustrations for the book were produced by the tremendously gifted Mike Samuelsen. Additional graphics, the Breakpoint website, and related marketing materials for the book were produced by a number of incredibly talented individuals: Don Berkman, Bernice Brennan, Chad Buechler, Tatiana Camacho-Daniel, Melissa Halim, Jordana Haspel, Brittany Johnson, Samantha Lim, Dustin Luther, Catherine Mangan, Brandon Mills, Mike Samuelsen, Lauren

Simpson, Alexander Staikos, and Sam Yacov. This team was led by Judy Hackett and Liz Gengl, both of whom I owe much gratitude. Particular thanks as well to my agent, Jim Levine, who has now shepherded me through two successful books. My first book was edited and published by the fantastic team at Harvard Business Press, and I owe a special thank you to them for allowing me to reuse and adapt some material that appeared previously in *Wired for Thought*.

In many respects, I tried to take readers of *Breakpoint* to the intersection of the brain, biology, and technology. As a result, I relied on a number of experts in those fields to help guide my writing. They include Paul Allopenna, Jim Anderson, Dan Ariely, Dan Dennett, Andrew Duchon, Carl Dunham, Deborah Gordon, David Landan, George Miller, Steve Reiss, and John Santini.

I owe a debt of gratitude to the entire team at the Dun & Bradstreet Credibility Corporation but in particular to the senior team—Bill Borzage, Sue Collyns, Pete Delgrosso, Hari Ganapathy, Judy Hackett, Wisdom Lu, Chris Nowlin, Sam Paisley, Aaron Stibel, and Gonzalo Troncoso—who put up with me while I was working on the book during many nights and weekends. I also want to thank Great Hill Partners in general and my board in specific (Michael Kumin and Chris Gaffney, as well as Peter Garran and Chris Skarinka). They encouraged me to complete *Breakpoint* in part because they knew it would improve our business: the partners at Great Hill are the rarest type of investors who understand the benefits of stepping back to gain perspective.

Nothing that I do would be possible without the support of my family. Thank you to my mom, dad, Aaron, Travis, Kristen, and Rick for always being there. I owe my wife and kids a particular thanks. Cheryl read numerous drafts of the book, and my 5- and 7-year-old children, Dennett and Lincoln, sat through two hour-long presentations on the subject and managed to provide a surprisingly critical review. My family contributed significantly to the book, but more importantly, they contribute significantly to my life.

APPENDIX

Matt Ridley (@MattWRidley)

The Defense Advanced Research Projects Agency (@Darpa)

Discovery News (@Discovery_News)

Harvard Business Review (@HarvardBiz)

National Science Foundation (@NSF)

Nature (@NatureMagazine)

Popular Science (@PopSci)

ScienceDaily (@ScienceDaily)

SciAm Mind (@SciAmMind)

Scientific American (@SciAm)

TechCrunch (@TechCrunch)

Wired (@Wired)

Wired Science (@WiredScience)

OTHERS NOT ON TWITTER AND WEBSITES OF INTEREST:

Association for the Advancement of Artificial Intelligence
http://www.aaai.org

BrainGate
http://www.BrainGate.com

Malcolm Gladwell
http://www.gladwell.com

Deborah Gordon's Lab
http://www.stanford.edu/~dmgordon/

E.O. Wilson's Foundation
http://www.eowilsonfoundation.org

Harvard Center for Brain Science
http://cbs.fas.harvard.edu/

Internet World Stats
http://www.internetworldstats.com

Naked Pizza
http://www.nakedpizza.biz

The Singularity
http://www.singularityu.org

Stanford's Neurogrid Project
http://www.stanford.edu/group/brainsinsilicon/neurogrid.html

TED
http://www.ted.com

WordNet
http:/wordnet.princeton.edu

NOTES

CHAPTER 1 - INTRODUCTION | REINDEER | NETWORKS

The most comprehensive account of the St. Matthew Island reindeer was written by David R. Klein of the Alaska Cooperative Wildlife Research Unit at the University of Alaska. He attributes the reindeer collapse to overconsumption as well as an extremely harsh winter in 1963–1964. See "The Introduction, Increase, and Crash of Reindeer on St. Matthew Island," *Journal of Wildlife Management* 32, no. 2 (1968): 350–367. A more recent review of the lichen in the area is provided in Stephen S. Talbot, Sandra Looman Talbot, John W. Thomson, and Wilfred B. Schofield, "Lichens from St. Matthew and St. Paul Islands, Bering Sea, Alaska," *Bryologist* 104, no. 1 (2001): 47–58.

There has been some recent debate among scientists as to which had a greater impact, the weather or the reindeer population, but the general consensus continues to be that the reindeer overconsumed and overshot their environment. For a contrary viewpoint, see the November–December 2009 article in *Weatherwise*, "What Killed the Reindeer of Saint Matthew Island?," by David Klein, John Walsh, and Martha Shulski.

‖

Robert F. Bruner states in *Deals from Hell: M&A Lessons That Rise above the Ashes* that only 13 percent of the 501 companies listed in the NYSE in 1925 still existed in 2004 (Hoboken, N.J.: Wiley, 2005), 1–2. That number is almost certainly lower now.

III

It should come as no surprise that Darwin plays a central role in most of the theory throughout this book. One of Darwin's most important points is often either misunderstood or completely ignored. He made it very clear that there is no such thing as "good or bad" when it comes to evolution, stating that "there is a frequently recurring struggle for existence, it follows that any being, if it vary however slightly in any manner profitable to itself, under the complex and sometimes varying conditions of life, will have a better chance of surviving, and thus be *naturally selected*." See *On the Origin of Species—A Facsimile of the First Edition* (Cambridge: Harvard University Press, 1964), p. 5. People often mistake this thought as a reason to believe that Mother Nature has a hand in what we humans define as progress. Stephen Jay Gould eloquently explained this in *Full House: The Spread of Excellence from Plato to Darwin* (New York: Harmony Books, 1996), p. 63: "Evolution, to us, is a linear series of creatures getting bigger, fancier, or at least better adapted to local environments." But "natural selection talks only about adaption to changing local environments . . . no feature of such local adaptation should yield any expectation of general progress." Gould also noted that written in Darwin's personal journal were the words "never say higher or lower."

CHAPTER 2 – ANTS | ANTERNETS | MANURE

Information about harvester ants comes from conversations with Deborah Gordon, her two books, and her numerous journal articles. Gordon's books are *Ant Encounters: Interaction Networks and Colony Behavior* (Princeton: Princeton University Press, 2010) and the earlier *Ants at Work: How an Insect Society is Organized* (New York: W. W. Norton, 2000). Her journal articles can be found on her Stanford University web page. For a general overview, Dr. Gordon gave an impassioned speech during the 2003 TED Conference entitled "The Emergent Genius of Ant Colonies," which can be found at http://www.ted.com/talks/deborah_gordon_digs_ants.html. Note the HREF tag "Deborah Gordon digs ants," which I thought was interesting enough that I repeated it in the first line of chapter 2. TED, which stands for "Technology, Entertainment, Design," is a global set of conferences created to disseminate ideas.

For a more general overview of ants, also see Edward O. Wilson and Bert Hölldobler's *The Ants* (Cambridge, Mass.: Harvard University Press, 1990); and Edward O. Wilson's *The Insect Societies* (Cambridge, Mass.: Harvard University Press, 1971) and *The Social Conquest of Earth* (New York: Liveright, 2012).

I

Many general interest books on the brain are worth reading, although none that I know of compare the brain to ants. For a general overview, see *How the Mind Works* by Steven Pinker (New York: W. W. Norton, 1997), *Consciousness Explained* by Dan Dennett (Boston: Little, Brown, 1991), *Principles of Psychology* by William James (Cambridge, Mass.: Harvard University Press, 1983), and *In Search of Memory: The Emergence of a New Science of Mind* by Eric Kandel (New York: W. W. Norton, 2006).

The Deborah Gordon quote comparing ant communication to Twitter messages comes from an article by Molly Vorwerck, "Deciphering Ant Communication," *The Stanford Daily*, November 16, 2010.

The phenomenon of ants circling until they die is discussed in Frédéric Delsuc's article, "Army Ants Trapped by Their Evolutionary History," *PLoS Biology* 1, no. 2 (2003): e37.

The quote in which Deborah Gordon discusses hassling ant colonies comes from her TED talk, mentioned above.

II

Dan Dennett compared the internet to an alien invasion when he was interviewed by Dr. David G. Stork and Michael O Connell for the documentary *2001: Hal's Legacy*. The interview is entitled "Evolution Intelligence: Daniel C. Dennett Interview."

Internet statistics change as rapidly as they are published, but two of the best sources are Internet World Stats, which tracks the world's internet usage (http://www.internetworldstats.com), and Netcraft, which does a monthly survey to estimate the number of websites on the internet. The most recent survey can be found at http://news.netcraft.com /archives/category/web-server-survey.

Wikipedia estimates that in 2007, YouTube alone consumed as much bandwidth as the entire internet did in 2000. YouTube provides its own statistics at http://www.youtube.com/t/press_statistics.

The *Washington Post* reported Netflix statistics on May 17, 2011: "Video Viewing on Netflix Accounts for up to 30 Percent of Online Traffic" by Cecilia Kang.

ZDNet announced in 2011 that "Facebook Is Bigger than the Whole Internet Was in 2004."

Source for mobile traffic growth comes from Cisco Visual Networking Index: "Global Mobile Data Traffic Forecast Update, 2012–2017."

To discover the similarities between ant communication and the internet's TCP, Deborah Gordon worked with Stanford computer scientist Balaji Prabhakar. The resulting paper, "The Regulation of Ant Colony Foraging Activity without Spatial Information," was published in the August 23, 2012, issue of *PLoS Computational Biology.*

For more information on how the brain uses a process similar to TCP to limit the flow of information, see Rene Marois and Jason Ivanoff's journal article, "Capacity Limits of Information Processing in the Brain," *Trends in Cognitive Sciences* 9, no. 6 (2005): 296–305; and also an article by The Physics arXiv Blog, "New Measure of Human Brain Processing Speed," *MIT Technology Review,* August 25, 2009.

III

Neuroscience is truly an evolving field, and because it is so new, information tends to be sparse or becomes out of date very quickly. I discuss the problem of finding accurate brain statistics further in chapter 10. Nonetheless, I have tried to use the most commonly cited statistics regarding the brain. For the number of neurons and connections in the human brain, I went with an adult mature brain having around 100 billion neurons and 100 trillion connections. It should be noted that recent research suggests the number of neurons may be around 86 billion, although this number is largely up for debate so I opted for the most conventional number throughout the book. For information on the latest research into the 86 billion theory, see Frederico A. C. Azevedo, Ludmila R. B. Carvalho, Lea T. Grinberg, José Marcelo Farfel, Renata E. L. Ferretti, Renata E. P. Leite, Wilson Jacob Filho, Roberto Lent, and Suzana Herculano-Houzel, "Equal Numbers of Neuronal and Nonneuronal Cells Make the Human Brain an Isometrically Scaled-up Primate Brain," *Journal of Comparative Neurology* 513, no. 5 (2009): 532–541. The number of neural connections is also contested, but the general consensus is 100 trillion connections. See, for example, Robert W. Williams and Karl Herrup,

"The Control of Neuron Number," *Annual Review of Neuroscience* 11 (1988): 423–453; Gordon M. Shepherd, ed., *The Synaptic Organization of the Brain* (New York: Oxford University Press: 2003); Narayanan Kasthuri and Jeff W. Lichtman, "Neurocartography," *Neuropsychopharmacology* 35, no. 1 (2010): 342–343; and Carl Zimmer, "100 Trillion Connections," *Scientific American* 304, no. 1 (2010): 58–63.

The number of neural connections in the brains of infants and children is even harder to determine accurately, but the consensus is that they peak at roughly 1,000 trillion neural connections. See, for example, Dennis Garlick, "Understanding the Nature of the General Factor of Intelligence: The Role of Individual Differences in Neural Plasticity as an Explanatory Mechanism," *Psychological Review* 109, no. 1 (2002): 116–136. The research shows that the number of neuronal connections decreases significantly from its childhood number, but again, sources vary as to how many connections are lost. For more information about the brains of infants and children, read *The Scientist in the Crib: What Early Learning Tells Us About the Mind* (New York: HarperCollins, 1999) by Alison Gopnik, Andrew N. Meltzoff, and Patricia K. Kohl.

Recent data have shown that neurons, not just neural connections, also decrease during adolescence. Lawrence K. Low and Hwai-Jong Cheng of the Center for Neuroscience at the University of California-Davis published their finding in 2006 that 50 percent of post-mitotic neurons do not survive until adulthood: "Philosophical Transactions of the Royal Society of London," Series B, *Biological Sciences* 361 (2006): 1531–1544. Also see J. A. Markam, J. R. Morris, and J. M. Juraska's "Neuron Number Decreases in the Rat Ventral, but Not Dorsal, Medial Prefrontal Cortex between Adolescence and Adulthood," *Neuroscience* 144 (2007): 961–968. Markam's research was also covered by *Science-Daily* on March 19, 2007, in their article, "The Brain Loses Neurons During Adolescence," written from materials provided by the University of Illinois at Urbana–Champaign. For more detail on the numbers of neurons and connections, see my book *Wired for Thought: How the Brain Is Shaping the Future of the Internet* (Boston: Harvard Business Press, 2009).

The amazing rate of neuronal growth of fetuses can be found in Ross A. Thompson's journal article, "Development in the First Years of Life," *The Future of Children* 11, no. 1 (2001): 21–33.

The extent to which ants and other eusocial insects collapse or prune their colonies is not well understood. It is clear that for each species, there is a breakpoint at which the colony stops growing, but no one has investigated the extent to which it overshoots first or the reasons that it does. It should also be noted, as Dr. Gordon has pointed out to me, that in these cases, it is not the environment that the animals are overshooting—that would, of course, lead to a total collapse, similar to what happened with the St. Matthew Island reindeer. Instead, they are likely overshooting some other natural equilibrium point, a topic we return to later in the book.

The data about the number of devices connected to the internet come from Cisco's 2011 white paper entitled "The Internet of Things: How the Next Evolution of the Internet is Changing Everything," which can be downloaded at cisco.com. For an impressive visual representation of the internet of things, including cows and farmers, see Cisco's infographic at http://share.cisco.com/internet-of-things.html.

The reindeer data used to create Image 2.3 are from David R. Klein's article, "The Introduction, Increase, and Crash of Reindeer on St. Matthew Island," *Journal of Wildlife Management* 32, no. 2 (1968): 350–367.

The MySpace data used to create Image 2.3 are from the article, "The Rise and Inglorious Fall of MySpace," by Felix Gillette, which appeared in *Bloomberg BusinessWeek* on June 22, 2011. Additional MySpace data were gathered from MySpace's Wikipedia article. The rise in number of links on the homepage was calculated by using the Wayback Machine at web.archive.org to look at older versions of MySpace.

Whether the ant or the colony is an organism has been discussed often in science and literature. Edward O. Wilson and Bert Hölldobler have a nice history of this debate in *The Ants*.

IV

The story about the nineteenth-century horse problem in New York City has been told numerous times, most recently in *Superfreakonomics: Global Cooling, Patriotic Prostitutes, and Why Suicide Bombers Should Buy Life Insurance* by Steven D. Levitt and Stephen J. Dubner (New York: William Morrow, 2009). I relied principally on details from the Living City Archive at Columbia University (livingcityarchive.org), the Sirolli Institute (sirolli.com), as well as a November 16, 2009, *New*

Yorker article entitled "HOSED: Is There a Quick Fix for the Climate?" Additional information on the history of New York City comes from a November 15, 1880, *New York Times* article entitled "The City's Sanitary Work."

Consumption estimates for the internet come from the aforementioned Cisco white paper, "The Internet of Things."

CHAPTER 3 – CANNIBALS | BRAINS | INTERNETS

For a general overview of Easter Island, see *Inventing "Easter Island"* by Beverly Haun (Toronto: University of Toronto Press, 2008). For a detailed discussion of the overshoot of Easter Island, see Jared Diamond's *Collapse: How Societies Choose to Fail or Succeed* (New York: Penguin, 2006).

I

For an interesting discussion about the brain's energy consumption, see Nikhil Swaminathan's article, "Why Does the Brain Need So Much Power?," *Scientific American,* April 29, 2008, which references this study: Fei Du, Xiao-Hong Zhu, Yi Zhang, Michael Friedman, Nanyin Zhang, Kâmil U_urbil, and Wei Chen, "Tightly Coupled Brain Activity and Cerebral ATP Metabolic Rate," *Proceedings of the National Academy of Sciences* 105, no. 17 (2008): 6409–6414.

The 20 percent number is widely recognized. See Marcus E. Raichle and Debra A. Gusnard, "Appraising the Brain's Energy Budget," *Proceedings of the National Academy of Sciences* 99, no. 16 (2002): 10237–10239.

II

There is no shortage of quality sources for the history of the internet, but a unique perspective worth reviewing comes from Internet Society: http://www.internetsociety.org/internet/what-internet/history-internet/brief-history-internet. Also of note is *Tubes: A Journey to the Center of the Internet* (New York: Ecco, 2012), in which author Andrew Blum recounts his fascinating journey through the wires of the internet.

The "internet of things" has received much attention as of late. In addition to the aforementioned Cisco white paper and infographic,

McKinsey & Company published a report in 2010 called "The Internet of Things." The *Economist* published a special report in the November 4, 2010, issue called "Augmented Business" with the subheading "Smart Systems Will Disrupt Lots of Industries, and Perhaps the Entire Economy."

III

For Metcalfe's grave predictions about the internet, see "What's Wrong with the Internet: It's the Economy, Stupid," *IEEE Internet Computing*, March/April 1997. Also of note is a speech Metcalfe gave in 2006 entitled "Framing the First Massachusetts Energy Summit." Transcript reprinted online at http://vcmike.wordpress.com/2006/12/15/guest-blogger-bob-metcalfe-on-framing-the-first-massachusett-energy-summit.

IV

For a more in-depth look of the theory of how cooking drove our intelligence, see Richard Wrangham's book *Catching Fire: How Cooking Food Made Us Human* (New York: Basic Books, 2009). Herculano-Houzel's findings were published in the *Proceedings of the National Academy of Sciences* in 2012 in an article co-written with Karina Fonseca-Azevedo entitled "Metabolic Constraint Imposes Tradeoff between Body Size and Number of Brain Neurons in Human Evolution." Herculano-Houzel, it should be noted, is the same person who discovered that we may have fewer than 100 billion neurons in our brain. Her findings came as a result of investigating the metabolic rates of consumption in the brain. For a brief overview of the findings of Richard Wrangham and Suzana Herculano-Houzel, see "Raw Food Not Enough to Feed Big Brains," by Ann Gibbons in the October 22, 2012, edition of the journal *Science Now*.

V

The 2 percent consumption number comes from a report by Greenpeace released in 2011. They detailed the energy use of major internet companies and rated each on its level of environmental friendliness. The interactive report is available at www.greenpeace.org.

Google was tight-lipped for years about its energy usage but finally disclosed statistics in September 2011. The *New York Times* presented these stats in a September 8, 2011, article entitled "Google Details, and

Defends, Its Use of Electricity" by James Glanz. Information about Google's carrier hotel can be found in "Google to Buy New York Office Building," *Wall Street Journal,* December 3, 2010.

George Miller's article about the limits of short-term memory is well worth reading: "The Magical Number Seven, Plus or Minus Two: Some Limits on Our Capacity for Processing Information," *Psychological Review* 63, no. 2 (1956): 81–97.

A brief overview of the growth of content-delivery networks and the scale at which they operate can be found in an article by Mari Sibley, "The Incredible Shrinking Internet," which appeared in *SmartPlanet* on June 20, 2012.

Neuroscience has known about the fallibility of neurons for several decades, but the exact failure rate is unknown. The following two sources estimate that neurons fail to fire between 50 and 75 percent of the time: Alex M. Thomson, "Facilitation, Augmentation and Potentiation at Central Synapses," *Trends in Neurosciences* 23, no. 7 (2000): 305–312; and William B. Levy and Robert A. Baxter, "Energy-Efficient Neuronal Computation via Quantal Synaptic Failures," *Journal of Neuroscience* 22, no. 11 (2002): 4746–4755. A more recent figure was given in *Discover* magazine on November 6, 2009, in the article, "Brain-Like Chip May Solve Computers' Big Problem" by Douglas Fox. This article pegged the failure rate at 30 to 90 percent, an even bigger range (and higher maximum failure rate) than previously established.

The Neurogrid chip was featured in the aforementioned October 2009 *Discover* magazine article. The most recent scientific data were presented by Swadesh Choudhary, Steven Sloan, Sam Fok, Alexander Neckar, Eric Trautmann, Peiran Gao, Terry Stewart, Chris Eliasmith, and Kwabena Boahen in their article, "Silicon Neurons that Compute," presented at the *International Conference on Artificial Neural Networks* in 2012. Additional information on Stanford's Neurogrid project can be found on the following website: http://www.stanford.edu/group/brainsinsilicon/neurogrid.html.

CHAPTER 4 – SLAVES | NEURONS | THE WEB

Howard Topoff has published several influential articles about the behavior of slave-making ants, including "Slave-Making Ants" in *American*

Scientist 78, no. 6 (November–December 1990): 520–528; and "Colony Founding by Queens of the Obligatory Slave_making Ant, Polyergus breviceps: The Role of the Dufour's Gland," co-written with Stefan Cover, Les Greenberg, Linda Goodloe, and Peter Sherman in *Ethology* 78, no. 3 (1988): 209–218.

For more information about slave-making ants, I would refer you again to Bert Hölldobler and Edward O. Wilson's *The Ants* (Cambridge, Mass.: Harvard University Press, 1990). For a general overview, see R. Deslippe's article, "Social Parasitism in Ants," published in *Nature Education Knowledge* 3, no. 10 (2010): 27.

I

Much of this section, specifically the information on how ideas leap from one brain to another, comes from Richard Dawkins's insight of a meme—an idea that behaves similarly to a gene—first discussed in *The Selfish Gene* (New York: Oxford University Press, 1976). Dawkins defines a meme as "an idea, behavior or style that spreads from person to person within a culture." Despite the title of the book, Dawkins makes a subtle yet critical point: that higher level biological systems can act selflessly despite having underlying selfish genes. This theory can explain how kin and other related parties can be altruistic, as they are protecting the greater species or underlying genes. There is some debate about certain details of kin selection, and Edward O. Wilson (who recently argued against natural selection in the journal *Nature*) and Dawkins are in the middle of an academic argument regarding the outcome. (See Nowak, Martin A., Corina E. Tarnita, and Edward O. Wilson, "The Evolution of Eusociality," *Nature* 466, no. 7310 (2010): 1057–1062.) Regardless, the selfish gene theory speaks to how ideas can act selfishly and propagate; it also explains how neurons can act selflessly and commit cellular suicide, a topic that is expanded upon throughout this chapter.

The quote from Deborah Gordon is from *Ant Encounters: Interaction Networks and Colony Behavior* (Princeton: Princeton University Press, 2010).

II

The story of Jill Price is nothing short of fascinating, and numerous articles have been written about her. The original journal article (with

Price's name redacted) can be found here: E. S. Parker, L. Cahill, and J. L. McGaugh, "A Case of Unusual Autobiographical Remembering," *Neurocase* 12, no. 1 (February 2006): 35–49. For a more personal account, see the book Price coauthored with Bart Davis: *The Woman Who Can't Forget: The Extraordinary Story of Living with the Most Remarkable Memory Known to Science—A Memoir* (New York: Free Press, 2008).

III

It is interesting to see the massive number of zeros that makes up a zettabyte, which you can view on a Wikipedia page dedicated to the number: wikipedia.org/wiki/Zettabyte.

The web stats are from Nielsen and Pew Research Center and include the fact that we each view 2,600 web pages and 90 sites per month. *Huffington Post* published an infographic by Visual Economics, which used this data in the article, "Internet Usage Statistics: How We Spend Our Time Online," by Catharine Smith, published June 22, 2010.

IV

The full bibliographical information for the articles and books named in this section are as follows: Nicholas Carr, "Is Google Making Us Stupid?," *The Atlantic,* July/August 2008; Nicholas Carr, *The Shallows: What the Internet Is Doing to Our Brains* (New York: W. W. Norton, 2010); Larry Rosen, *iDisorder: Understanding Our Obsession with Technology and Overcoming Its Hold on Us* (New York: Palgrave Macmillan, 2012); Daniel Sieberg, *The Digital Diet: The 4-Step Plan to Break Your Tech Addiction and Regain Balance in Your Life* (New York: Three Rivers Press, 2011); Dr. Kimberly Young, *Caught in the Net: How to Recognize the Signs of Internet Addiction—and a Winning Strategy for Recovery* (New York: John Wiley & Sons, Inc., 1998); and *Tangled in the Web: Understanding Cybersex from Fantasy to Addiction* (Bloomington, IN: AuthorHouse, 2001).

V

The *USA Today* article about the size of the web, entitled "Internet Suffering from Information Overload," was written by Andrew Kantor and published on June 14, 2007.

The over 800 percent growth in the number of websites figure comes from a study by Edward T. O'Neill, Brian F. Lavoie, and Rick Bennett, "Trends in the Evolution of the Public Web 1998–2002," *D-Lib Magazine* 9, no. 4 (2008): 1–10. The number 19 percent is from data available for 2011 and 2012 from Netcraft's "Web Server Survey," which is published every month and available at news.netcraft.com.

Neilson reported in 2012 that fewer people used the web on their PCs in 2012 than in 2011, the first year that this has happened. I expect this number will continue to decline. Read "State of the Media: The Social Media Report 2012" by Nielsen for more details. The article can be downloaded at neilson.com, but you must register first.

Data firm Flurry also released stats in December 2012 showing an increase in app usage and a decline in the amount of time people spent using the web on PCs (from 72 minutes in 2011 to 70 minutes in 2012). Their data is a composite from comScore, Alexa, and the US Bureau of Labor Statistics. See TechCrunch's article, "Time Spent in Mobile Apps Is Starting to Challenge Television, Flurry Says," by Kim-Mai Cutler and published on December 5, 2012. Note that this is the source for the data used in Image 4.1.

Chris Anderson published an article in *Wired* magazine in 2010 with the headline, "The Web Is Dead. Long Live the Internet." The headline and commentary was prescient but the stats were unfortunately wrong. He leveraged a graph from Cisco which showed the web in decline since 2000 but the decline was a result of breaking out different components of the web, such as video. He was deeply criticized—in particular by Tim O'Reilly and John Battelle—for the blunder. Battelle summarized it well by stating, "As a last word, I'd like to say that if the scope of the piece was really just about the web as a viable model for 'professional content' as we see it, then splashing 'The Death of the Web' on the cover might be, well, overstating the case just a wee bit . . ." Fast forward to today and the web is in decline but even with that news, it is not dying; it is growing stronger.

CNN reported on January 28, 2011, in an article entitled "108 Apps per iPhone" by Philip Elmer-DeWitt about the mobile usage stats presented in this section, which were derived from an Appsfire infographic about app usage. Appsfire found that the average iPhone user has 108 apps and spends 84 minutes a day using them. The Flurry data, discussed above, found that smartphone owners use apps for 127 minutes per day. I used the latter 127 minutes figure because it is a more current source.

In another highly relevant white paper that can be downloaded at cisco.com, "Cisco Visual Networking Index: Global Mobile Data Traffic Forecast Update, 2011–2016," Cisco predicted that global mobile data traffic will increase by a factor of 18 by 2016.

VI

A similar approach to what I am describing is the semantic web, which has been proposed by World Wide Web founder Tim Berners-Lee. The problem with the semantic web, however, is in both the limitation of its scope and the difficulty of actually implementing it. Berners-Lee first proposed the idea in 2001, and we still have not made significant progress toward those goals, as Berners-Lee has indicated over the years. See Tim Berners-Lee, James Hendler, and Ora Lassila, "The Semantic Web," *Scientific American* 284, no. 5 (2001): 28–37.

VII

The quote about electricity comes from "Nature's Revenge on Genius," *Nature: A Weekly Journal for the Gentleman Sportsman, Tourist and Naturalist,* vol 1, no. 1 (November 2, 1889), Nature Publishing Group.

CHAPTER 5 – BREAD | MOBILE | SOCIAL

The bread distribution story was recounted in Paul Seabright's masterpiece about economic networks, *The Company of Strangers: A Natural History of Economic Life,* 2nd ed. (Princeton: Princeton University Press, 2010). A slightly different version of the story was presented by Jonas Eliasson at a September 2012 TED conference.

I

Tom Anderson, who called himself "Lord Flathead," was a computer hacker from the tender age of 13. Many articles have been written about his early days, including a comprehensive one by Michael Arrington of *Tech Crunch* entitled "MySpace Cofounder Tom Anderson Was a Real Life 'WarGames' Hacker in the 1980s," printed in August 30, 2008.

This section references *Wired for Thought: How the Brain Is Shaping the Future of the Internet* (Boston: Harvard Business Press, 2009).

II

The original research for Robin Dunbar's number was on primates: "Neocortex Size as a Constraint on Group Size in Primates," *Journal of Human Evolution* 20 (1992): 469–493. Dunbar later went on to write a book that went into deeper detail: *Grooming, Gossip, and the Evolution of Language* (Cambridge, Mass.: Harvard University Press, 1998). His work on human social networks is summed up in this article: "Social Network Size in Humans," *Human Nature* 14, no. 1 (2003): 53–72. A number of great studies have applied Dunbar's number to the internet in general and to social networks in particular. See Bruno Goncalves, Nicola Perra, and Alessandro Vespignani, "Modeling Users' Activity on Twitter Networks: Validation of Dunbar's Number," *Bulletin of the American Physical Society* 57, no. 1 (2012); or Russell Hill, R. Alexander Bentley, and Robin Dunbar, "Network Scaling Reveals Consistent Fractal Pattern in Hierarchical Mammalian Societies," *Biology Letters* 4, no. 6 (2008): 748–751.

Edison Research found in June 2012 that the average Facebook user has 262 friends. Their report is called "The Social Habit 2012."

The network of the brain is built on clusters of neurons, each tightly connected. These clusters then connect to other clusters and eventually form one network composed of many subnetworks—a "network of networks." The beauty of the brain is that it allows the overall network to grow while maintaining equilibrium within its subnetworks. This is very similar to the strategy that Facebook employed in the early days of the network's growth.

Facebook's web versus mobile stats, as well as the other social networks, are from the aforementioned Nielsen social media report.

Writer Paul Boutin outlined new features released for Facebook's mobile interface in a January 2, 2013, article in the *New York Times* entitled "More Facebook Changes, Aimed at Users on the Go."

Google's Horowitz made his remarks during a 2012 conference in New York City. It was reported on by Steve Kovach in *Business Insider* on November 28, 2012, in his article entitled "The Google+ Boss Just Brilliantly Deconstructed Everything Annoying About Facebook."

Mark Zuckerberg's quote about Instagram comes from an April 9, 2012, *New York Times* article entitled "Facebook Buys Instagram for

$1 Billion" by Evelyn M. Rusli. *New York Times* pulled the quote from Zuckerberg's Facebook profile page.

III

The always insightful Kevin Kelly has several great TED talks. If you only watch one, my favorite is "The Next 5,000 Days of the Web" from 2007, where this quote comes from.

Stories of social media gaffes are literally everywhere you look. The story of a Canadian woman named Nathalie Blanchard who lost her disability benefits was reported by Ki Mae Heussner of *ABC News* on November 23, 2009: "Woman Loses Benefits after Posting Facebook Pics." *Mashable* reported on June 28, 2010, "Facebook Becoming a Prime Source for Divorce Case Evidence." The *Washington Post*'s Katie Rogers reported "Kenneth Cole's Egypt Tweet" on February 3, 2011. The *New York Times* reported on the Domino's video prank on April 15, 2009 ("Video Prank at Domino's Taints Brand"), and *USA Today* reported on Taco Bell's beef lawsuit on April 21, 2011 ("Yum Execs: Lawsuit Still Hurting Taco Bell Sales).

CHAPTER 6 – CHIEFS | SEARCH | CONTEXT

Information about Marisa Mayer and her career history can be found at http://www.biography.com/people/marissa-mayer-20902689.

Mayer's quote comes from Bernard Girard's book *The Google Way: How One Company Is Revolutionizing Management as We Know It* (San Francisco: No Starch Press, 2009).

I

Information on the history of Yahoo! can be found on their website at http://docs.yahoo.com/info/misc/history.html or on Wikipedia. The *Wall Street Journal* also has a nice timeline and infographic called "The Story of a Struggling Internet Pioneer" published on July 17, 2012.

Number of pages added to the web is reported by Google and can be found at: http://googleblog.blogspot.com/2008/07/we-knew-web-was -big.html.

Wikipedia has by far the most comprehensive overview of Google Search, with a litany of references. For history buffs and tech geeks, an original article on Google PageRank can be found at Stanford: http://infolab.stanford.edu/~backrub/google.html.

The full bibliographies for the books noted in this section are Terry Winograd, *Understanding Natural Language* (Academic Press, 1972); *Language as a Cognitive Process* (Boston: Addison-Wesley, 1983); and *Understanding Computers and Cognition* (Boston: Addison-Wesley, 1987).

III

Irina Slutsky reported that 358 out of approximately 3,600 Facebook employees used to work at Google in her June 1, 2011, article in *AdAge,* "Meet the Ex-Googlers Running Facebook."

For more on what happened with Facebook's Beacon, check out *PC Magazine's* November 2007 article, "Facebook's Beacon More Intrusive Than Previously Thought." You can also view Mark Zuckerberg's mea culpa when the company agreed to take down the service as a result of the backlash: https://blog.facebook.com/blog.php?post=10150378701937131.

Kevin Kelly's quote comes from the above referenced 2007 TED talk, "The Next 5,000 Days of the Web."

IV

Mayer's quote comes from an article in the November 2009 *PCWorld* article entitled "Google VP Mayer Describes the Perfect Search Engine"

CHAPTER 7 – CROWDS | POETS | SHAKESPEARE

Harvard historian Robert Darnton wrote an entire book about "The Affair of the Fourteen." It's a work of impressive scholarship that also happens to be highly entertaining: *Poetry and the Police: Communication Networks in Eighteenth-Century Paris* (Cambridge, Mass.: Belknap Press of Harvard University Press, 2010).

II

For more information on the chronometer competition—called the Longitude Prize—visit the National Museum of the Royal Navy at http://www.royalnavalmuseum.org/info_sheets_john_harrison.htm. DesignCrowd also created an infographic about crowdsourcing throughout history that can be viewed at http://blog.designcrowd.com/article/202/crowd

sourcing-is-not-new—the-history-of-crowdsourcing-1714-to-2010. The group rightly points out that even reality TV shows like *American Idol* are, in essence, crowdsourced contests.

The *Guardian* reported about the slowdown and breakpoint of Wikipedia, with some of the stats used in this chapter in the November 25, 2009, article by Jack Schofield, "Have You Stopped Editing Wikipedia? And If So, Is It Doomed?" No surprise, but the best information on Wikipedia is on Wikipedia. You can read more about Wikipedia's current size and past growth in its article, "Wikipedia: Size of Wikipedia." http://en.wikipedia.org/wiki/Wikipedia:Size_of_Wikipedia. Wikipedia's strategic plan is available for review at http://wikimediafoundation .org/wiki/Wikimedia_Movement_Strategic_Plan_Summary. For an interesting discussion of Wikipedia's future, see the *Wall Street Journal* classroom edition article from January 2010, "What's Wrong with Wikipedia?" by Julia Angwin and Geoffrey A. Fowler.

Stats on the *Encyclopedia Britannica,* as compared to Wikipedia, come from "Wikipedia: Size Comparisons" from Wikipedia. The graph data come from "Wikipedia: Modelling Wikipedia's Growth" from Wikipedia. More information about the various ways to graph Wikipedia's growth can be found on that page.

Quote from the *Encyclopedia Britannica* CEO comes from the *New York Times* March 14, 2012, article by Julie Bosman entitled "MEDIA DECODER; Britannica Is Reduced to a Click."

Quotes from Wikipedia board member Mathias Schindler and Carnegie Mellon professor Aniket Kittur come from the aforementioned January 2010 *Wall Street Journal* article by Julia Angwin and Geoffrey A. Fowler entitled "What's Wrong With Wikipedia?"

For more information about Jorge Cauz and his transformation of Encyclopaedia Britannica for the internet age, see the article he wrote for the March 2013 issue of *Harvard Business Review* entitled "Encyclopaedia Brittanica's President on Killing Off a 244-Year-Old Product."

III

The story of James Murray and his role in the creation of the *Oxford English Dictionary* is available in—where else?—the *Oxford Dictionary of National Biography* (http://www.oxforddnb.com/public/dnb/35163 .html), and also in a January 13, 2011, *Wired Magazine* article by Nate Lanxon entitled "How the Oxford English Dictionary Started out Like

Wikipedia." For a more nuanced account, see Simon Winchester's *The Professor and the Madman: A Tale of Murder, Insanity, and the Making of the Oxford English Dictionary* (New York: Harper Perennial, 2005). The quote about the idea behind the *Oxford English Dictionary* is found in the preface to volume 1.

James Surowiecki's *The Wisdom of Crowds* (New York: Anchor Books, 2004) is a fascinating look into the ways in which crowds are better than experts.

IV

ODesk facts and figures can be found on the company's website. Both GE and Netflix have extensive materials on their respective websites about the crowdsourced prizes they offer.

V

The details and results of Karen Klein's bullying crowdsourcing campaign can be seen in the *Huffington Post* in "Karen Klein Donations: Indiegogo Campaign Ended Friday with $703,873," published on July 20, 2012.

David Carr wrote an article on political crowdsourcing and social media entitled "How Obama Tapped into Social Networks' Power" for the *New York Times* on November 9, 2008.

In its December 2012 article, "Crowdfunding Will Make 2013 the Year of the Gold Rush," *Forbes Magazine* predicts that crowdfunding in the United States, which raised nearly $3 billion in 2012, will skyrocket in 2013, likely hitting the $6 billion mark by the end of the year.

Kickstarter reported on its website that Amanda Palmer was the first musician to raise over $1,000,000.

VI

The crowdsourced novel was covered by *Time* magazine on April 29, 2012, in the article, "Would You Read a Crowdsourced Novel?" by Heba Hasan.

CHAPTER 8 – SQUIRTS | PROFIT | TRAFFIC

I first heard of the sea squirt phenomena from Dan Dennett, who also briefly mentioned it in his book *Consciousness Explained* (Boston:

Little, Brown, 1991). The sea squirt is explained more broadly in a psychological context in a July 2012 *Psychology Today* article by Sian Beilock, "How Humans Learn: Lessons from the Sea Squirt." A contrarian viewpoint, arguing that sea squirts don't actually eat their brains, can be found at *Fast Company* in a surprisingly rich April 1999 article by Lisa Chadderdon called "Brainless Fish in Topless Bar." The counterargument is that a portion of the brain is digested, not literally eaten. Regardless of the semantics, the point is still clear: if something is costly and not useful, it will be selected out (or eaten).

I

Proganochelys (Greek for "early turtle") is the official name of these ancient turtles from the late Triassic period. They look like modern turtles except for their spiked necks and tails.

The relatively lightweight internal structure of sharks makes it easier for them to stay buoyant and means that they require less energy to swim than they would if they had heavier bones. Here, again, we see that evolution favors energy efficiency throughout nature.

II

Duke University's Dan Ariely and his colleagues have shown that people do not behave rationally when things are offered for free. Ariely devotes a full chapter to the topic in his book *Predictably Irrational: The Hidden Forces That Shape Our Decisions* (New York: HarperCollins, 2009). See also Kristina Shampanier, Nina Mazar, and Dan Ariely, "Zero as a Special Price: The True Value of Free Products," *Marketing Science* 26, no. 6 (2007): 742–757. For a general interest overview, see Daniel Kahneman's *Thinking Fast and Slow* (New York: Penguin, 2011).

Drs. Ilias Leontiadis and Christos Efstratiou from the Computer Science Laboratory at the University of Cambridge conducted the study of free versus paid apps. They surveyed apps on the Android platform, though it's reasonable to guess that numbers would be similar for all smartphone users. Their research focused on privacy concerns: they found that free apps request more permissions (and are more invasive—such as asking for a user's friends list and contact info) than paid apps. They concluded that the price of a free app may not be exactly free after all. See Ilias Leontiadis and Christos Efstratiou, "Don't Kill My Ads!: Balancing Privacy in an Ad-Supported Mobile Application Market," in

Proceedings of the Twelfth Workshop on Mobile Computing Systems &
Applications, p. 2. ACM, 2012.

There are many different sources and much folklore for the success
rate of a venture fund, just as there are many numbers for the success
rates for start-ups and small businesses. Because many of these investors
and businesses are private, there is no good source to reference. For the
book, I went with a general average, but feel free to review "The Venture
Capital Secret: 3 Out of 4 Start-Ups Fail" by Deborah Gage in the *Wall
Street Journal* from September 19, 2012.

See George Nichols's discussion of Webvan and Peapod's respective
values in his 1999 article "Can Webvan Milk a Profit?," *Morningstar,*
November 12, 1999. Peapod's announcement of shipping costs was covered by Barry Janoff, "Peapod Delivers New Shipping Costs," *Adweek,*
August 22, 2001.

In *The Innovator's Dilemma: The Revolutionary Book That Will
Change the Way You Do Business* (New York: HarperCollins, 2000),
Clayton Christensen notes the idea that sometimes a company can kill
its bigger competitor by doing something less well. He says, "Occasionally disruptive technologies emerge—innovations that result in worse
product performance, at least in the near term . . . generally disruptive
technologies underperform established products in mainstream markets. But they have other features . . . they are typically cheaper, simpler,
smaller, and frequently, more convenient to use." While price does not
work well for start-ups as a competitive differentiator in mature markets
(where the product will be seen as cheap), it can be used effectively in the
growth phase of an emerging market as a competitive strategy.

III

Stephen Budiansky wrote a detailed article called "The Physics of Grid-
lock" about the science of traffic jams for *The Atlantic* in December 2000.

Jonas Eliasson outlined the concept of a traffic tax in his 2012 TED
talk, "How to Solve Traffic Jams." Scientific results can be found in
his articles, "Lessons from the Stockholm Congestion Charging Trial,"
Transport Policy 15, no. 6 (2008): 395–404; and "Do Cost-Benefit
Analyses Influence Transport Investment Decisions? Experiences from
the Swedish Transport Investment Plan" co-authored with Mattias Lun-
dberg in *Transport Reviews* 32, no. 1 (2012): 29–48. Also of interest

may be one of his original articles proposing the idea prior to the institution of the tax, "Transport and Location Effects of Road Pricing: A Simulation Approach," *Journal of Transport Economics and Policy* 35, no. 3 (2001): 417–456.

IV

Tech bloggers were up in arms about Facebook's charging $100 to message Mark Zuckerberg. The least alarmist articles were the best ones, including this one by Matthew Lynley: "Mystery Solved: Why It Costs $100 to Send Mark Zuckerberg a Facebook Message," *Wall Street Journal,* January 11, 2013.

Google's financial tables can be viewed at http://investor.google.com/financial/tables.html.

The story of Nick Bergus's joke about personal lubricant that turned into a Facebook ad was reported by Somini Sengupta in an article entitled "On Facebook, 'Likes' Become Ads," in the *New York Times,* May 31, 2012.

For an interesting article about more private social networks, such as Edmodo, that cater to educators, see Jason Tomassini's "Social Networks for Teachers on the Rise As Popular Social Media Raise Concerns," *Huffington Post,* January 8, 2013.

Naked Pizza is one of the best recent case studies of a company that leveraged social media with truly astounding results. Read how the founders did it in Fawn Fitter's 2010 article, "The Sizzling Success Of Naked Pizza," *Entrepreneur,* October 8, 2010.

LinkedIn noted on its website in January 2013 that it had surpassed 200 million users. Many of Reid Hoffman's investments can be seen on his LinkedIn or CrunchBase profile.

CHAPTER 9 – PHEROMONES | LANGUAGE | MIRRORS

Most of the discussion of ant pheromones comes from Deborah Gordon's *Ant Encounters: Interaction Networks and Colony Behavior* (Princeton: Princeton University Press, 2010).

The Vanderbilt study mapping out the ant's 400 different olfactory receptors was reported by various outlets; see, for example, "Ants Have Exceptionally 'Hi-Def' Sense of Smell," *Science Daily,* September 10, 2012.

The Language Log at the University of Pennsylvania notes that the online *Roster of Programming Languages* lists 8,512 computer languages (http://languagelog.ldc.upenn.edu/nll/?p=1467). They joke about how someone was able to count all of the programming languages, but there is some truth to their point. I suspect that number, while as good as any, is not terribly credible. The author, Stanford linguist Arnold M. Zwicky, estimates that the number is at least 7,000.

I

Ed Stabler's comments about the demand for linguists were found in "Linguists Suddenly 'Hot' Hires in Dot.Com World" published on October 10, 2000, by *UCLA Today*, which is a magazine for UCLA faculty and staff.

II

While the precise time periods are not known, the language acquisition critical development periods are reasonably well understood. Articles used here include: Christophe Pallier, "Critical Periods in Language Acquisition and Language Attrition," in *Language Attrition: Theoretical Perspectives,* ed. Barbara Köpke, Monika S. Schmid, Merel Keijzer, and Susan Dostert (Amsterdam and Philadelphia: J. Benjamins, 2007), 155–168; Susan J. Hespos, "Language Acquisition: When Does the Learning Begin?", *Current Biology* 17, no. 16 (2007): R628–R630; and Stephen D. Krashen, "Lateralization, Language Learning, and the Critical Period: Some New Evidence," *Language Learning* 23, no. 1 (1973): 63–74.

Steven Pinker's quote comes from *The Language Instinct* (New York: William Morrow, 1994).

The quote from David Birdsong and the data for the accompanying figure come from his article, "Interpreting Age Effects in Second Language Acquisition," in *Handbook of Bilingualism: Psycholinguistic Approaches,* ed. Judith F. Kroll and Annette M. B. DeGroot (New York: Oxford University Press, 2005), 109–127.

III

A portion of this section, as well as section V, comes from prior work, including my previous book *Wired for Thought: How the Brain Is Shaping the Future of the Internet* (Boston: Harvard Business Press, 2009), as well as work performed by Jim Anderson, George Miller, Steve Reiss,

Dan Ariely, Paul Allopenna, Carl Dunham, Andrew Duchon, David Landan, John Santini, and the entire brain science team at Simpli.

George Miller unfortunately passed away in 2012, but his work can still be found at Princeton: http://www.cs.princeton.edu/~rit/geo. For more detailed information on WordNet, see *WordNet: An Electronic Lexical Database,* edited by Christiane Fellbaum with a preface by George Miller (Cambridge, Mass.: MIT Press, 1998).

Steven Pinker's quote comes from his book *How the Mind Works* (New York: W. W. Norton, 1997).

The seminal work on spreading activation comes from Allan M. Collins and Elizabeth F. Loftus, "A Spreading-Activation Theory of Semantic Processing," *Psychological Review* 82, no. 6 (1975): 407–428.

The ad with the woman stuffed into a suitcase was referenced from Stefanie Olsen, "Automated Search Ads Can Boomerang," *CNET News,* September 26, 2003.

IV

You can learn more about Giacomo Rizzolatti's research and how he discovered mirror neurons by visiting his academic website at http://www.unipr.it/arpa/mirror/english/staff/rizzolat.htm. Rizzolatti's story was retold by Sandra Blakeslee in "Cells That Read Minds," *New York Times,* January 10, 2006.

V. S. Ramachandran's quote about mirror neurons appeared in his January 2006 *Edge* article, "Mirror Neurons and the Brain in the Vat."

USC neuroscientist Michael Arbib's quote comes from James R. Hurford, "Language beyond Our Grasp: What Mirror Neurons Can, and Cannot, Do for the Evolution of Language," in *Evolution of Communication Systems* (Cambridge, Mass.: MIT Press, 2004), 297–314.

V

Elkhonon Goldberg's quotes come from *The Wisdom Paradox: How Your Mind Can Grow Stronger As Your Brain Grows Older* (New York: Gotham Books, 2005).

VI

Devavrat Shah's critique of Netflix was published in an article by Chris Matyszczyk, "MIT Prof: Netflix Has Its Recommendations Wrong," *CNET,* July 11, 2011.

Other info about the Netflix algorithm, including the quote from the Netflix algorithm team, comes from Xavier Amatriain and Justin Basilico, "Netflix Recommendations: Beyond the 5 stars," *The Netflix Tech Blog,* June 20, 2012.

An interesting spin on the Netflix Prize winners and new contest is presented by Michael V. Copeland, "Box Office Boffo for Brainiacs: The Netflix Prize," *CNN Money,* September 21, 2009.

The Forrester Research study that estimated as much as 60 percent of Netflix recommendations turn to sales was reported by JP Mangalindan, "Amazon's Recommendation Secret," *CNN Money,* July 30, 2012.

Information on Amazon's collaborative filtering comes in part from Greg Linden, Brent Smith, and Jeremy York of Amazon.com through an industry report by the *IEEE Computer Society,* January/February 2003 entitled "Amazon.com Recommendations: Item-to-Item Collaborative Filtering."

Quote from *Fortune* about the Amazon recommendation engine comes from JP Mangalindan's article, "Amazon's Recommendation Secret," from the July 2012 issue.

An account of YouTube's switch to Amazon's algorithms can be found in this article: James Davidson, Benjamin Liebald, Junning Liu, Palash Nandy, Taylor Van Vleet, Ullas Gargi, Sujoy Gupta et al., "The YouTube Video Recommendation System," *Proceedings of the Fourth ACM Conference on Recommender Systems* (2010): 293–296.

Chris Anderson wrote about Jeff Bezos's desk in "The Zen of Jeff Bezos," *Wired Magazine,* January 2005.

Netflix's new social media "mirror neurons" were reported on by Xavier Amatriain and Justin Basilico on the Netflix website in an article entitled "Netflix Recommendations: Beyond the 5 Stars (Part 2)" in June 2012.

Amazon's human "mirror neurons" were reported on by JP Mangalindan in the above-referenced *Fortune* article.

CHAPTER 10 – EEG | ESP | AI

The September 2010 article by Kathleen McAuliffe, "If Modern Humans Are So Smart, Why Are Our Brains Shrinking?" in *Discover* magazine gives an interesting overview of anthropologist John Hawks's findings about our shrinking brain. It is also worthwhile to look at the following study by two developmental psychologists, D. H. Bailey and D. C. Geary, which is referenced in the article, "Hominid Brain Evolution: Testing Climactic, Ecological, and Social Competition models," *Human Nature* 20 (2009): 67–79.

I

Peter H. Lindert and Jeffrey G. Williamson showed that the industrial revolution brought a twofold increase in wealth: "English Workers' Living Standard During the Industrial Revolution: A New Look," *Economic History Review* 36 (1983): 1–25. Various population sources show a fourfold increase in the world's population, the effects of which are discussed by Erin McLamb, "The Ecological Impact of the Industrial Revolution," *Ecology,* September 18, 2011.

II

For a brief but relevant summary of the scientific achievements of Hans Berger, see the National Institutes of Health's review entitled "Neurological Stamp" at http://www.ncbi.nlm.nih.gov/pmc/articles /PMC1738204/pdf/v074p00009.pdf. Berger's story has been retold by many, most notably in Dean Radin's interesting book *Entangled Minds: Extrasensory Experiences in a Quantum Reality* (New York: Paraview, 2006), 21–24.

E. E. Fetz reported his findings in "Operant Conditioning of Cortical Unit Activity," *Science* 163 (1969): 955–958. For a more in-depth look at brain computer interfaces in general, see *Brain-Computer Interfaces: Applying Our Minds to Human-Computer Interaction* (New York: Springer, 2010), edited by Desney S. Tan and Anton Nijholt.

III

The *60 Minutes* segment featuring Jan Scheuermann is well worth watching as is the original BrainGate segment, both of which can be found on the CBS website. Alternatively, you can read a good description of the breakthrough in "Patient Shows New Dexterity with a Mind-Controlled Robot Arm" by Susan Young in the December 2012 *MIT Technology Review.*

IV

For more information on any of the brainwave sensor companies mentioned in this section, see their websites or search for neurowear.

The full bibliographies for the two articles about Zeo's headband are as follows: Scott Kirsner, "A Gentler Way to Start the Day," *Boston Globe,* March 28, 2005; and David Pogue, "To Sleep, Perchance to Analyze," *New York Times,* July 15, 2009.

Tesla's story was featured on NPR's *All Things Considered* in a piece entitled "Tesla's Big Gamble: Can the Electric Car Go Mainstream?," which aired September 24, 2012.

V

In Homer's *Iliad,* Hephaestus was the god of artisans and blacksmiths. He was a smith who made gold statues to serve as his handmaidens, as well as three-legged wheeled cauldrons that traveled to and from the other gods at a nod from him.

Robots programmed for the workplace are particularly interesting. In addition to delivering mail and getting coffee, the HRP-4 can be programmed to recognize co-worker's faces. The downside is that it costs $350,000. Not to be outdone, the slightly more expensive PR2 can also get you food from the refrigerator. The iRobot Roomba can be found for under $100. A fun overview was provided by *Bloomberg Businessweek* in "The Robot in the Next Cubicle" on January 14, 2011.

Kevin Kelly wrote a great piece about robots for *Wired Magazine* on December 24, 2012: "Better Than Human: Why Robots Will—And Must—Take Our Jobs." The figure that machines have taken all but 1 percent of agricultural jobs is from this article.

This section references Richard Dawkins's *The Blind Watchmaker* (New York: W. W. Norton, 1987).

My previous book *Wired for Thought: How the Brain Is Shaping the Future of the Internet* (Boston: Harvard Business Press, 2009) provides a more detailed review of Gammonoid, Big Blue, and all the other intelligent, game-playing machines.

The 100 billion neurons theory is extremely well researched and notably quoted in *The Scientific American Book of the Brain* (New York: Scientific American, 1999). The following journal article does a good job outlining that research, as well as detailing new evidence about the 86 billion neuron theory: F. A. C. Azevedo, L. R. B. Carvalho, L. T. Grinberg, J. M. Farfel, R. E. L. Ferretti, R. E. P. Leite, W. J. Filho, R. Lent, and S. Herculano-Houzel, "Equal Numbers of Neuronal and Nonneuronal Cells Make the Human Brain an Isometrically Scaled-up Primate Brain," *Journal of Computational Neurology* 513 (2009): 532–541. Alternatively, *The World Book 2001* (Chicago: World Book Inc., 2001), 551, quoted a number between 10 billion and 100 billion. The only safer estimate would have been to estimate the number at between zero and 1 trillion.

The Dan Dennett quote about reverse engineering comes from an interview at *Edge* entitled "The Normal Well-Tempered Mind" on January 8, 2013.

VI

John von Neumann was a brilliant mind by any definition. He was a mathematician but made contributions to fields as diverse as computer science, the humanities, physics, economics, and statistics. He also worked on the Manhattan Project to develop the first nuclear bomb and was appointed to the Institute for Advanced Studies at Princeton alongside Albert Einstein. Much of his writing about computers focused on biological similarities and analogies. He wrote a book called *The Computer and the Brain* (New Haven, Conn.: Yale University Press, 1958), in which he first mentioned the concept of a singularity. The first use of the word, however, came prior to von Neumann from science fiction writer Vernor Vinge.

This section references Ray Kurzweil's *The Singularity Is Near: When Humans Transcend Biology* (New York: Viking, 2005).

CHAPTER 11 – CONCLUSION | TERMITES | EXTINCTION

There are many works on the nests of the leaf-cutter ants, including the comprehensive work by Bert Hölldobler and Edward O. Wilson, *The Leafcutter Ants: Civilization by Instinct* (New York: W. W. Norton, 2011).

A fascinating documentary featuring Bert Hölldobler called "Ants: Nature's Secret Power" contains impressive footage of the excavation of a large leaf-cutter mound and is available in its entirety on YouTube. The Hölldobler quote in this chapter comes from this documentary.

The biologists working on the Brazil site mentioned in this chapter include Aldenise A. Moreira and Luiz Carlos Forti. Of the several articles they published on their findings with numerous colleagues, the following article was primarily used: Aldenise Moreira, Luiz Carlos Forti, Ana Paula Andrade, Maria Aparecida Boaretto, and Juliane Lopes, "Nest Architecture of Atta laevigata (F. Smith, 1858) (Hymenoptera: Formicidae)," *Studies on Neotropical Fauna and Environment* 39, no. 2 (2004): 109–116.

Termites are very similar to ants in many respects. References used in this section include these five: (1) Eric E. Porter and Bradford A. Hawkins, "Latitudinal Gradients in Colony Size for Social Insects: Termites and Ants Show Different Patterns," *The American Naturalist* 157, no. 1 (January 2001): 97–106; (2) J. M. Dangerfield, T. S. McCarthy, and W. N. Ellergy, "The Mound-Building Termite *Macrotermes michaelseni* as an Ecosystem Engineer," *Journal of Tropical Ecology* 14 (1998): 507–520; (3) Dini M. Miller, "Subterranean Termite Biology and Behavior," *Virginia Cooperative Extension,* Publication 444–502 (2010); (4) Ulrich G. Muller, Nicole M. Gerrardo, Duur K. Aanen, Diana L. Six, and Ted R. Schultz, "The Evolution of Agriculture in Insects," *Annual Review of Ecology, Evolution, and Systematics* (2005): 563–595; and (5) Roger E. Gold, Harry N. Howell, Jr., Grady J. Glenn, and Kimberly M. Engler, "Subterranean Termites," *Texas A&M System AgriLife Extension E-Publication,* December 2005.

You can see pictures of, and obtain more information about, the incredible Eastgate Centre at the architect's website, http://www.mick pearce.com.

I

This section references *Connected: The Surprising Power of Our Social Networks and How They Shape Our Lives—How Your Friends' Friends' Friends Affect Everything You Feel, Think, and Do* (New York: Little, Brown, 2009) by Nicholas Christakis and James Fowler.

The essay "I, Pencil" by Leonard Read was originally published in the December 1958 issue of *The Freeman*. Today you can read it online.

The Matt Ridley quote is from yet another great TED talk, "When Ideas Have Sex." It was given at the TEDGlobal 2010 Conference.

Many animals are "social," but very few are "eusocial," including humans, ants, and termites. Biologists have divided animals into various social levels including presocial, subsocial, parasocial (which can include communal, quasisocial, and semisocial animals), and eusocial, which is the highest level of sociality.

Mark Moffett's quote about the similarities between humans and ant colonies is from Jennifer Viegas's article, "Human Societies Starting to Resemble Ant Colonies," published by *Discovery News* on May 2, 2012.

II

Jared Diamond's *Collapse: How Societies Choose to Fail or Succeed* (New York: Penguin, 2006) is referenced in this section. Additionally, see his essay, "The Worst Mistake in the History of the Human Race," *Discover Magazine* (May 1987): 64–66.

AFTERWORD: THE INTERNET IS A BRAIN

The Internet is a brain was the main topic of my 2009 book *Wired for Thought: How the Brain Is Shaping the Future of the Internet* (Boston: Harvard Business Press). In the book, I outlined a path toward creating a thinking and conscious internet, which I have summarized here. Portions of this appendix come from that book, with the courtesy of Harvard Business Press. More detailed notes are available in *Wired for Thought*.

I

Purdue University psychologist James Townsend provides a fun and insightful account of the distinction between serial and parallel processing in the brain and outlines why it is so important. While it is a scientific paper, it is relatively accessible: "Serial vs. Parallel Processing: Sometimes They Look Like Tweedledum and Tweedledee but They Can (And Should) Be Distinguished," *Psychological Science* 1, no. 1 (January 1990): 46–54.

II

Quotes from Dan Dennett in sections II and III come from *Consciousness Explained* (Boston: Little, Brown, 1991).

III

Howard Margolis's quote comes from his book *Patterns, Thinking, and Cognition: A Theory of Judgment* (Chicago: University of Chicago Press, 1988).

Douglas Hofstadter's ingenious book *I Am a Strange Loop* (New York: Basic Books, 2007) does a remarkable job of describing parallel processing as a recursive process similar to the feedback of a speaker when a microphone is too close or a series of mirrors that reflect infinitely into one another. Hofstadter states it this way: "In the end, we are self-perceiving, self-inventing, locked-in mirages that are little miracles of self-reference."

In *Outliers: The Story of Success* (New York: Little, Brown, 2008), Malcolm Gladwell argues that great success is composed of two components: The first is luck, or timing. The second is practice, which, in many ways, is the mind's way of automating its strange loop.

IV

The 500,000 dopamine neurons number is, like all neuronal figures, a guess. Neuronbank.org estimates it is between 400,000 and 600,000, referencing two respectable sources: (1) A. Bjorkland and S. Dunnett, "Dopamine Neuron Systems in the Brain: An Update," *Trends in Neuroscience* 30, no. 5 (2007): 194–202; and (2) S. Chinta and J. Andersen, "Dopaminergic Neurons," *The International Journal of Biochemistry & Cell Biology* 37 (2005): 942–946.

The example of a cup of coffee spinning in mental rotation comes from Read Montague, *Your Brain Is (Almost) Perfect: How We Make Decisions* (New York: Plume, 2006), 83.

Plato presented his theory of forms in several of his works. It is covered most extensively in *Republic*, Book III, V, VI–VII, and IX–X.

Steven Pinker's quote comes from *How the Mind Works* (New York: W. W. Norton, 1997).

Daniel Goleman's quote comes from *Emotional Intelligence* (New York: Bantam, 1995), 15–17.

V

The quote from Doug Lenat comes from an interview with Jeffrey Goldsmith published in *Wired Magazine* in April 1994 with the title "CYC-O."

The Erik Schmidt quote was originally written in a letter to George Gilder of *Wired Magazine* back in 2003 and reprinted in an October 2006 article in *Wired* entitled "The Information Factories."

Researchers reported on Spaun in a 2012 *Science* article by Chris Eliasmith, Terrence C. Stewart, Xuan Choo, Trevor Bekolay, Travis DeWolf, Charlie Tang, and Daniel Rasmussen entitled "A Large-Scale Model of the Functioning Brain," *Science* 338, no. 6111 (November 30, 2012): 1202–1205. You can also read about Spaun in Rebecca Boyle's article, "Meet Spaun, the Most Complex Simulated Brain Ever," *Popsci*, November 29, 2012, which is the source of the quote from Chris Eliasmith. Also see Francie Diep's article, "Artificial Brain: 'Spaun' Software Model Mimics Abilities, Flaws of Human Brain," *Huffington Post*, November 29, 2012.

John Markoff wrote about how entrepreneurs are using data to mine human intelligence in "Entrepreneurs See a Web Guided by Common Sense," *New York Times*, November 11, 2006.

INDEX